THE BUSINESS LEGENDS OF INDIA

ARJUN SAMPAT

ISBN 979-8-89322-783-3

This book is dedicated to my parents **Dimple & Kaushal and my brother Dhruv**.

Thank you for the books, conversations, love and laughter.

Always together, through thick and thin!

TABLE OF CONTENTS

PREFACE

The Indian economy and business landscape have undergone a sea change since Independence in 1947. Looking back at the days of the License Raj when profit was considered to be a bad word, one wonders how Indian businesspeople succeeded at the time. The economy then threw off its shackles with the liberalization of the early 1990s and Indian businesses prepared themselves to compete with multinational companies. While there were many skeptics, Indian companies successfully integrated with the global economy and proved that they could hold their own in the international market.

The IT and ITeS boom of the 21st century was tailor-made for India. The country had a young population, skilled in math and computer science; the English language was widely used in India, our manpower costs were incredibly low and we were located in a very convenient time zone. It was no surprise that India became the back- office of the world.

Over the past few years, we have seen India reaping the fruits of the JAM trinity – Jan Dhan bank accounts for its vast unbanked population, Aadhar identity verification and Mobiles in every hand. The ubiquity of the internet and the lowest data costs in the world have made India a hub for innovation in the BFSI sector. India's Unified Payments Interface (UPI) is the world's largest real-time payment market and has enabled an explosion of e-commerce in India.

The Covid pandemic and geopolitical tensions between China and the Western world, have caused a conscious restructuring of global supply chains. MNCs are now moving to a China+1 strategy which means that they are looking to diversify their investments into countries other than China. India's manufacturing sector is bound to benefit from this.

It is an exciting time to be a young Indian entrepreneur. India is now the world's third largest start-up ecosystem after China and the US. We have 115 unicorns in India with a cumulative valuation of US$ 350 billion.

But who were the trailblazers who made India's growth story possible? What were their characteristics? What were the strategies they used to succeed? Who are today's business leaders and how are they driving growth in today's volatile world?

My book seeks to answer these questions. It is intended for students, young adults, and anyone who has an interest in exploring the journeys of India's leading entrepreneurs.

India aims at becoming a developed nation by 2047, the centenary year of its independence. Entrepreneurs will play a large role in helping the country achieve this goal. If my book inspires even a handful of its readers to become entrepreneurs, it will have served its purpose.

ARJUN SAMPAT

GAUTAM **ADANI**

Who is **Gautam Adani?**

Gautam Adani was born to a middle-class family on 24th June 1962 in Ahmedabad, Gujarat, one among eight siblings. His father Shantilal Adani was a small textile merchant. After his schooling, Gautam Adani enrolled for a B.Com degree in Gujarat University but dropped out in the second year because of his interest in business. Unwilling to join his father's textile business, he went to work as a diamond sorter for Mahendra Brothers in Mumbai in 1978. In a couple of years, he founded his own diamond trading firm and became a millionaire at age 20.

In 1981, his brother, Mansukh Adani bought a plastic factory in Ahmedabad and asked Gautam to help manage it. Here, Gautam became familiar with the import and trade of Polyvinyl Chloride (PVC), marking his entry into the global trading market. There was no looking back. He soon began importing primary polymers and established Adani Exports in 1988.

Economic liberalization in the early 1990s enabled Adani Exports (later renamed as Adani Enterprises Ltd) to diversify, becoming a trading conglomerate dealing in coal, commodities, and agro-products.

Gautam Adani diversified into ports by establishing the Mundra Port and today Adani Ports and SEZ (APSEZ) is India's largest port operator. Adani is also the country's largest private airport operator. Adani Power was founded in 1996 and is the largest private thermal power producer in India.

Today, the Adani Group is a conglomerate involved in renewable power, solar manufacturing, power generation, transmission and distribution, gas distribution, mining, cement, transportation and logistics, infrastructure, media, real estate, financial services and edible oils & food.

Forbes estimates Gautam Adani's net worth to be US$ 79.9 billion.

AWARDS AND RECOGNITION

- Gautam Adani received the USIBC Global Leadership Award in 2022
- Awarded the Ramakrishna Bajaj Memorial Global Award in 2021
- Received the Gujarat Law Society Institute of Business Management's Excellence in Management Award in 2007

KEY STRATEGIES AND
SUCCESS FACTORS

Acquisition: In order to create a strong presence in any sector in a short period of time, strategic acquisitions are important. Gautam Adani has mastered the use of mergers & acquisitions. The Adani Group's acquisition of Ambuja and ACC Cement from the Holcim Group in 2022 made it India's second largest cement producer. In 2022, the Adani Group also acquired India's leading media company NDTV. The Adani Group also acquired the Haifa Port in Israel in February 2023.

Focus on Infrastructure Building: Gautam Adani believes that there are great opportunities for building world class infrastructure in India since the country faces a significant infrastructure deficit. He has driven the Adani Group's rapid growth by diversifying into the infrastructure sector and focusing on it, particularly ports, airports and transport infrastructure.

Diversification into Adjacent Domains: Gautam Adani's diversification is largely driven by his belief in investing in areas that are adjacent to the Group's current businesses. For example, after succeeding in power generation, Adani Group moved into transmission and distribution of power. Entry into adjacent domains has helped the Adani Group grow rapidly.

ANIL AGARWAL

Who is **Anil Agarwal?**

Anil Agarwal was born in 1954 in Patna, Bihar and attended school there. His father ran a small aluminium conductor business. After finishing school, Anil Agarwal joined this business instead of going to college. Eventually, he left this too, arriving in Mumbai at age 19 to try his luck, bringing almost nothing with him.

Initially, he started as a scrap metal dealer operating from a tiny office with a rented telephone, buying scrap from cable companies in various states and selling to buyers in Mumbai. He then managed to get a bank loan to buy Shamsher Sterling Corporation, a manufacturer of enamelled copper. In 1986, he started manufacturing jellyfilled cables by setting up a factory for INR 70 million (US$ 5 million), which was significantly less than the conventional INR 300–400 million that it would cost. This company was called Sterlite Industries.

A few years into the business, Anil Agarwal wanted better control over raw material prices i.e., copper and aluminium, both of which were highly volatile. He set up India's first copper smelter and refinery in the private sector. He then commissioned plants to manufacture aluminium sheets, foils and optical fibre. The Government of India wanted to privatise its mining assets and Anil Agarwal was a very keen bidder. His Group (now known as Vedanta) acquired 38.8 percent interest in India Foils Ltd, 51 percent interest in Bharat Aluminium Co Ltd (BALCO) and 46 percent interest in Hindustan Zinc Ltd. He then integrated backwards into bauxite mining and exploration. Today, Vedanta Ltd is India's largest, and one of the world's leading producers of aluminium. Group company Cairn Oil & Gas is India's largest private sector crude oil producer.

Anil Agarwal then relocated to London where the world's mining and metal giants have their headquarters. In 2003, he listed Vedanta Group on the London Stock Exchange (LSE), establishing the group as a global player in mining and metals. In 2007, Anil Agarwal went on to list Sterlite Industries on the New York Stock Exchange (NYSE). Today, Vedanta Group is a global natural resources conglomerate with operations in India, South Africa, Liberia, Namibia.

In 2021, he signed the Giving Pledge, promising to give away 75% of his wealth to charity.

Forbes estimates Anil Agarwal's net worth to be US$2.01 billion.

KEY STRATEGIES AND
SUCCESS FACTORS

Backward Integration: With his sharp entrepreneurial mind, Anil Agarwal has always recognised that backward integration was critical to keep costs low in his business. This is the genesis of Vedanta Group's journey from cables to smelting, refining and mining.

Valuing your Team: Anil Agarwal credits his team for a lot of his success. He says, "No matter how far you get in life, you must always take your people with you. Whether it is your CEO or your factory worker on the ground, you must empower your people to deliver their best."

Acquisitions: Anil Agarwal is well known for using acquisitions to expand the Vedanta Group. His acquisition of BALCO, HZL and India Foils during the Government's privatisation drive is a good example. Other key acquisitions were Sesa Goa (at that time India's largest producer of iron ore) in 2007 and Cairn India (India's largest private sector producer of crude oil) in 2011. Acquisitions have been a key part of Anil Agarwal's playbook in India and Africa.

AWARDS AND RECOGNITION

- Anil Agarwal received The Economic Times, Business Leader Award in 2012
- Received the Mining Journal Lifetime Achievement Award in 2009
- Bestowed the Ernst & Young (EY) Entrepreneur of the Year award in 2008
- Received the Asian Awards Entrepreneur of the Year in 2016
- Received the Dr. Thomas Cangan Leadership Award from the Faculty of Management Studies, Institute of Rural Management, Jaipur in 2013
- Bestowed the Lifetime Achievement Award at The Asian Achievers Awards in 2019
- Awarded the Asian Business Philanthropy Award in 2021
- Received the Canada-India Foundation Global Indian Award in 2022

DHIRUBHAI **AMBANI**

Who is **Dhirubhai Ambani?**

Dhirubhai Ambani was born on 28th December 1932, in the state of Gujarat. Dhirubhai was the third of five children born to a village schoolteacher and his wife. He had a very modest upbringing and studied up to Grade 10. After this, Dhirubhai migrated to join his brother in Aden, Yemen at the age of 17 to serve as a clerk in an international trading firm A. Besse & Co. His monthly salary at that time was INR 300. He then moved to the commodities section of the firm, handling petroleum products for Shell, a reputed MNC. It was here that Dhirubhai garnered skills in commodity trading and accounting.

In 1958, he returned to India and set up a spice trading business, calling it Reliance Commercial Corporation, with an investment of INR 15,000. Soon he expanded into other commodities as well, growing the business rapidly by offering higher quality products at lower profit margins. He soon moved into the lucrative, yet risky business of yarn trading. He began the process of backward integration by setting up Reliance's first synthetic fabrics mill in Naroda, Gujarat producing textiles under the 'Vimal' brand. Reliance Commercial Corporation was now renamed Reliance Textiles Engineering Pvt. Ltd, which in turn was renamed Reliance Industries Ltd in 1973.

Dhirubhai kickstarted the equity cult in India by launching the company's IPO in 1977 which was oversubscribed seven times. Given the large number of retail shareholders, Dhirubhai used to conduct Reliance's Annual General Meetings in sports stadiums to accommodate all of them.

Continuing to integrate the business backwards, Dhirubhai gradually shaped Reliance into a petrochemicals and plastics behemoth. He also diversified into the telecom and power generation industries.

When Dhirubhai passed away on 6th July 2002 at age 69, the Reliance Group was valued at US$ 15 billion, a testimony to the vision of the man who built it.

AWARDS AND RECOGNITION

- Dhirubhai Ambani received India's second highest civilian award, the Padma Vibhushan posthumously in 2016
- Received the Dean's Medal from The Wharton School, University of Pennsylvania for Leadership in 1998
- Received the Economic Times Lifetime Achievement Award for Corporate Excellence
- Conferred Man of the Century award by Chemtech Foundation and Chemical Engineering World in recognition of his outstanding contribution to the growth and development of the chemical industry
- Named the "Man of 20th Century" by the Federation of Indian Chambers of Commerce and Industry (FICCI)

KEY STRATEGIES AND
SUCCESS FACTORS

Backward Integration: Backward integration was Dhirubhai's key strategy to drive Reliance's growth. Starting with textiles, he pursued a strategy of backward vertical integration - in polyester, fibre intermediates, plastics, petrochemicals, petroleum refining, and oil and gas exploration & production - to be fully integrated along the materials and energy value chain. This gave Dhirubhai control over cost, margins and quality.

Creating the Cult of Equity in India: Dhirubhai Ambani is credited with attracting the general public to the stock market in India. At a time when stock investments were limited only to the elite and businesspeople, Dhirubhai attracted 58,000 middle-class investors when he issued 2.8 million shares of Reliance at a cost of just INR 10 each in 1977. The Reliance AGM in 1985 was conducted in a football stadium in Mumbai and had more than 12,000 investors in attendance. Over the years, Reliance shareholders showered their trust and affection on Dhirubhai and he reciprocated by helping them build wealth.

Managing the Regulatory Environment: Dhirubhai Ambani was a master at managing the bureaucracy and Government. He famously said, "You have to sell your idea to the Government, and show how the company's plans fit in with national priorities." This strategy allowed him to get the Government's support and regulatory clearances required to drive Reliance's growth.

MUKESH **AMBANI**

Who is **Mukesh Ambani?**

Mukesh Ambani was born on 19th April, 1957 in Aden, Yemen to Kokilaben and Dhirubhai Ambani. He was one of four children. In 1958, the family shifted to Mumbai where Dhirubhai set up Reliance Commercial Corporation, the first step in building India's largest private corporation.

Mukesh earned a bachelor's degree in Chemical Engineering from the Institute of Chemical Technology (formerly UDCT), Mumbai. He later pursued an MBA from Stanford University but left the program in 1981 to join Dhirubhai at Reliance where he helped drive the company's background integration. Mukesh sought to build Reliance into India's first fully integrated private oil company, with its operations spanning oil & gas exploration, petroleum refining, petrochemicals, and retailing of petroleum products. To achieve this objective, he built Reliance's Jamnagar refinery which is today the world's largest and most complex single-site refinery. Even after the split of the Reliance business in 2006, Mukesh has gone from strength-to-strength diversifying and growing Reliance Industries Ltd into a Fortune 500 corporation and the largest private sector company in India.

Some highlights pertaining to Reliance:
- Reliance Retail is the country's largest and most profitable retail company across all formats.
- Reliance's telecom business Jio is the largest operator in India offering services such as connectivity, fibre, mobile devices, apps, etc.
- Reliance is investing US$ 10 billion in its New Energy business to create reliable, clean and affordable energy solutions with hydrogen, wind, solar, fuel cells, and batteries.
- Reliance's Media & Entertainment business is one of India's largest media houses with an omni- channel presence. It is among the top 10 digital publishers in the world.

Forbes estimates Mukesh Ambani's net worth to be US$ 110.6 billion.

AWARDS AND RECOGNITION

- Mukesh Ambani received the Ernst & Young (EY) Entrepreneur of the Year Award in 2000
- Received 'ET Business Leader of the Year' Award from The Economic Times in 2017
- Awarded the 'Othmer Gold Medal' from Chemical Heritage Foundation in 2016
- Bestowed the US-India Business Council (USIBC) 'Global Vision Award' for Leadership in 2007
- Conferred the Penn Engineering Dean's Medal for application of engineering & technology in 2010
- Received 'ET Business Leader of the Year' Award from The Economic Times in 2006
- Conferred the Asia Society Leadership Award in 2018
- Bestowed the India Business Leadership Award by CNBC-TV18 in 2007
- Conferred an honorary Doctor of Science degree by Institute of Chemical Technology, Mumbai

KEY STRATEGIES AND SUCCESS FACTORS

Choose the Right Businesses to be in: Mukesh Ambani applies very stringent criteria for selecting the businesses in which Reliance should enter. He looks for businesses where there is large pent-up and perpetual demand. This helps ensure that Reliance can enjoy a healthy annual growth rate over decades. Retail and telecom are very good examples of businesses that Reliance chose to enter because they met these criteria.

Focus on Greater Good: In a country like India which confronts many socio-economic challenges, Mukesh has always placed great importance of Reliance playing a large role in society. This is why Reliance seeks to provide extremely cost-effective solutions to consumers. For example, when Reliance Jio was launched, its low pricing helped drive digital penetration in the country. Before Jio's launch, India ranked 155th in mobile data consumption in the world but in less than a year after Jio's launch, India catapulted to number one. The low data prices helped benefit consumers and society, while simultaneously enabling Reliance to dominate the telecom sector. In addition to business, the not-for-profit Reliance Foundation, chaired by Nita Mukesh Ambani, focuses on meeting some of India's most pressing developmental challenges with innovative solutions. The Reliance Foundation is India's largest corporate foundation, having positively impacted the lives of over 70 million people.

Leverage Technology and Innovation : According to Mukesh, Reliance effectively leverages technology and innovation to disrupt sectors. Technology ensures that the company's business operations are digital, agile, and efficient, thus making them very cost competitive. Low pricing helps deliver higher market share, while cost-competitive solutions give Reliance industry-leading margins. These combine to enable Reliance create higher value.

NAKUL AGGARWAL & RITESH ARORA

Who are **Nakul Aggarwal & Ritesh Arora?**

Nakul Aggarwal and Ritesh Arora met as roommates while studying computer science at the Indian Institute of Technology, Bombay (IIT), amongst the top engineering colleges in India. After graduating, they could have easily taken up high paying jobs, but their heart was set on entrepreneurship.

Nakul and Ritesh founded a start-up in their final year at IIT, focused on sentiment analysis of products sold online. They were building a software layer on top of various online marketplaces to summarize customer sentiment about products. Unfortunately, they were ahead of their time in 2005; they pitched the idea to over 50 VCs but couldn't secure funding, so they dropped the idea. They needed to support themselves, so they took day jobs at Lime Labs LLC and worked there for three years.

However, the entrepreneurial fire was still burning. They founded another start-up, this time focused on information aggregation. The tool that they built got a lot of traction online; unfortunately, they couldn't monetize the idea and they shut it down in 2008.

After both start-ups failed, their families and friends suggested to Nakul and Ritesh that they build a consultancy business. The third start-up Downcase was a profitable venture and became their stepping stone to building BrowserStack. While creating Downcase's website, Nakul and Ritesh realized that it took longer to test the website on different browsers and operating systems, than to build it. They quickly researched the issue on social media and found that developers globally faced this problem. This was the genesis of BrowserStack in 2011.

Operating from a coffee shop, Nakul and Ritesh first developed free testing software for Internet Explorer. For feedback, they reached out to John Resig, Founder of jQuery. He loved the product and tweeted about it and within 3 weeks, BrowserStack accumulated 10,000 beta users. Next came monetization; they released a paid version after a couple of months and it saw great traction. In a year's time, BrowserStack generated revenue of US$ 1 million. The company has gone from strength-to-strength in the app and browser testing domain; it now offers testing on 3,000+ devices and browsers and is used by 50,000 customers globally.

Bootstrapped by Nakul and Ritesh for 6 years, BrowserStack first raised venture funding in 2018 from Accel. In 2021, it raised US$ 200 million in its Series B Round led by Bond and with participation from Insight Partners and Accel. In the process, BrowserStack became a SaaS unicorn with a valuation of US$ 4 billion.

Nakul and Ritesh are each estimated to have a net worth of over US 1.5 billion.

KEY STRATEGIES AND **SUCCESS FACTORS**

Learning from Mistakes: Nakul and Ritesh perceived their mistakes as opportunities to learn, rather than thinking of them as failures. They persevered even after two failed start-ups, applying the lessons that they learned to build BrowserStack into one of India's most valuable SaaS unicorns.

Financially Sustainable Business Model: To build BrowserStack, Nakul and Ritesh adopted a financially sustainable business model that generated revenue and profits. This financial discipline has helped them build a robust business that enjoys a great valuation.

Identifying a Large Problem to Solve: With their first two start-up ideas, Nakul and Ritesh attempted to create or introduce new concepts into the market. Unfortunately, these did not work. However, BrowerStack addressed a very large pre-existing problem in the digital market. Solving this massive problem faced by developers globally has helped BrowserStack to scale.

AWARDS AND RECOGNITION

- BrowserStack named Leader in G2's Grid® Report Winter 2023 in the Software Testing and Test Automation categories
- BrowserStack received the ET Start-up Award in the Bootstrap Champ Category in 2015
- The company was named in the Forbes Cloud 100, the definitive ranking of the top 100 private cloud companies in the world, in 2018 and 2021
- BrowserStack was named in the list of LinkedIn's 25 most attractive startups in India in 2018

NAKUL AGGARWAL

Q: Together with Mr. Ritesh Arora, you founded two start-ups, the first focused on sentiment analysis of customers and the second on information aggregation. Neither of these start-ups worked out – very often, entrepreneurs are dissuaded after failures. However, despite these failures you continued your dream of entrepreneurship and set up BrowserStack. Can you share your learnings from these failures and how you maintained your entrepreneurial ambitions despite them?

A: Our first start-up focused on customer sentiment analysis. Ritesh and I studied computer science at IIT Bombay and were very excited about technology, so we learned about amazing technologies in Artificial Intelligence (AI) back in 2006 and we actually ended up building a cool technology, not a cool product. So the key lesson learned from our first start up, is that you need to build a product, which solves a customer problem, and is not just a 'cool' technology.

The second start-up revolved around information aggregation and taught us the importance of having a strong business model. This start-up had a great product that was popular with a lot of users, however, there was no way to make a big business out of it; we could make some decent money from 'ads', but we didn't know back then on how to scale it. At the time, we didn't know about B2B as an opportunity. We were fresh graduates and were focused on developing a B2C product, but the space we had chosen for our second start-up was not suitable for a B2C business. So those were the two important learnings from our first two start-ups. Of course, we learned some other things as well, technology-related, but business-wise, those were the two important learnings.

And how did I maintain my entrepreneurial ambitions? I suppose we were very, very sure about making and doing something big out of India. Ritesh had an influence on me but together I think we wanted to prove that India can make global products.

We also realised that the product of our second start-up was actually good, so we were confident that we could build a sound product. But we just needed to figure out how to make a business out of that product and obviously make money as well.

Q: From studying your background, I learned that you and Ritesh are former IIT roommates and very close friends. Yet, both of you are also very different from each other. How do both of you constructively challenge yourselves? How has your relationship evolved as BrowserStack has grown and how do you handle disagreements?

A: I believe that differences of opinion are part and parcel of life (in all aspects).

And, we have had many :)

Looking back, in our early days we had our ups-and-downs because we were still figuring things out - both personally and professionally. But, 3 great learnings for us were:

1. Talk things out
2. Separate emotions and logic
3. Bifurcate professional and personal issues

We have been very tight since the beginning of time; our relationship has evolved over the years, and I think we call each other more than we call our wives and families. :)

We have been quite determined to bring up new ideas, reading and learning through the years, and discussing and brainstorming with each other. This is often accompanied by differences of opinion and different takeaways from the same business situation or article, and we challenge each other with reasonable arguments. Taking a step back and coming back with a better argument, sleeping over the other person's opinion - leads to better conversation the next day. But, aligning on 'one' thing and believing in it is extremely important (it's a different and more evolved version of a famous term: "disagree and commit").

Q: But how do you handle disagreements?
A: I think obviously that maturity has also filtered in, if there is a disagreement, we'll both take a back seat, rethink it, and then have a better conversation. More mature 'conversation' is the right word. But we still have disagreements on strategy, problem-solving, and our approach at times, and we probably iterate through it. And I think one thing that helps is that we are very clear about whose final decision it is because otherwise, we would end up in a situation where we cannot reach a conclusion. Having a crystal clear division of domains based on each one's strengths and then mutually agreeing or disagreeing on things, keeping each other's strong suits in mind always helps us arrive at the best decision on the whole. Also, my key learning is having differences eventually turns out better for us since it helps us view each option with an optimistic as well as pessimistic lens before reaching a conclusion. This process helps our relationship and also in reaching a better and more evolved answer/solution.

Q: BrowserStack has been commended for being a bootstrapped start-up for the first 6-7 years of its journey. I recall you saying that both Ritesh and you treated coffee shops around Mumbai as your workspaces in your initial years. How did you create a self-sustaining business model that permitted BrowserStack to increase in scale without outside investment? Were there any times when the future of the company didn't seem secure and that you and your employees were worried about the viability of your business?
A: From our first startup, where we couldn't

> *Having a crystal clear division of domains based on each one's strengths and then mutually agreeing or disagreeing on things, keeping each other's strong suits in mind always helps us arrive at the best decision on the whole.*

raise enough money - we learned the importance of being bootstrapped. All the venture capitalists (VCs) we spoke with mentioned the necessity of us having a user-base before they could invest in us. In our second start-up, we learned we needed to make some money to establish product-market fit to be attractive to potential investors.

So the third time around, from the get-go we had the clarity that we have to build a business that functions on its own. How did we create it? I think we spent a good amount of time on what our pricing model should be, and how we should go about making money. But I think the core driver of our success was that the problem we solved was a big pain-point for our user base of engineers, and they were very excited to see such a simple solution for their problem. This helped us in getting revenue off the bat, and then we scaled the business from there. I think B2B SaaS (business-to-business Software-as-a-Service) marked the turning point for BrowerStack. Moving to a SaaS model which we did within the first 6-9 months of launch, helped us in making the business more self-sustaining.

But was there any time when BrowserStack didn't seem secure? I don't think so; by God's grace, that didn't happen to us. I don't think we ever felt insecure from a revenue perspective. I think obviously it's a growth B2B tech business and you're always asymmetric in terms of performance.

So obviously there were times when the growth was not what we aspired for (and as founders, it was never good enough whatever it was) :). I think those were the stressful moments for us, but we never questioned the viability of the business.

Q: What coffee shops did you work in?
A: Always Costa Coffee because we used to like their coffee and there was no Starbucks in India, back then in 2011.

There was also Barista Coffee at the time, but somehow we always ended up being at Costa Coffee. Our most frequented outlet was the one near 7 Bungalows in Andheri West, Mumbai. I used to stay at 7 Bungalows and Ritesh used to stay close by in Lokhandwala Complex. We would alternate - one day at the Costa Coffee near 7 Bungalows, and the next day at the Costa Coffee outlet near Lokhandwala market junction. 80% of the time we did business in those two Costa Coffee outlets, because we wanted to optimise travel time, and it worked well for both of us to have the coffee shots rolling in for the kick we needed to get our work done real fast.

Q: Direct communication with customers on social media and other platforms helped BrowserStack gain traction and acceptance in the developer community. Now that you are a global company, how do you ensure that you remain in close touch with customers? How has BrowserStack adapted its structure to continue understanding customer needs in this growing market?
A: We spend a lot of time with our customers. I think this is extremely important for any business- to know what the customers' needs are, and how these are evolving. If I build a product today, the market is moving, so obviously I'm making sure my product is ready for the new, upcoming technology and market conditions. But the customers' needs are also changing because their businesses too are evolving in their own fields. So spending time with customers to understand whether our products meet their changing needs is extremely important and we dedicate a good amount of time to meet with them: either in person during our travels, or virtually through Zoom calls and other media. Hence, customer interaction is an important metric for both of us. In our

Objectives and key Results (OKRs), we have to meet X customers per quarter just to make sure we don't drop the ball there. In general, I think we are constantly in touch with our customers and that has remained a non-stop metric.

Additionally, we take customer support very seriously, especially all the support requests we receive from customers. In some product companies, support is sold as an add-on. At BrowserStack, we consider support as a core part of the product. So anyone who asks for support has to get the answer really fast. On top of that, we get a lot of queries. Do you support this? Do you not support this? Are you going to build this? And other such queries. For BrowserStack, the queries that users send are very useful in giving us direction, to understand where customers are going, and what we should be building next.

Q: BrowserStack aims to dominate the market for browser testing and has acquired several companies like Nightwatch in pursuit of this ambition. What will mainly drive Browserstack's growth in the future - organic growth driven by internal R&D or inorganic growth through acquisitions?

A: Both organic and inorganic growth. Organic growth because we are big believers that we can solve any engineering problem, maybe a little too optimistic since we have the best Talent... So I think we'll continue to grow organically and we also plan to build new product lines. We are already working on a few and look to continue adding more. As of now, we have five product lines and probably want to get to 20-25 product lines over the next two years. For this, our focus on internal Research and Development (R&D) is going to be the key. But I think if there's a good opportunity, we are extremely open to inorganic growth. That's an OKR for us as well, to get inorganic growth for BrowserStack.

Q: An important factor for BrowerStack's technological innovation is investing in talent. As you diversify your geographic presence and bring on talent in new markets, how do you ensure that BrowserStack's innovation-led culture transmits across borders? What strategies does BrowerStack use for global talent acquisition and what does the company look for in the large and highly competitive talent pool?

A: We are big believers that 'great people build great companies' and follow it in practice as well through our approach, systems, and policies.

How do we build an "innovation-led culture"? This is a hard problem to solve. Always a Work in Progress (WIP). Defining our value system, and keeping "innovation" and "problem-solving" at the forefront of individual evaluation ensures we don't let it dilute as we scale.

Following OKRs principally ensures people come up with great solutions to solve problems and we always focus on outcomes instead of effort.

Following repeatable templates and low-friction processes goes a long way to ensure new talent is focused on solving problems to grow the business, rather than getting lost in the "burden of scaled processes", of a mid-size organisation.

BrowserStack became a remote company during COVID in 2021 and we have a huge talent base across India. We have 900 employees working with us in 150+ cities/ towns in India. So that's huge and is working really well for us. Are we okay to have talent outside India? We have a presence in Dublin, Ireland, and in the US. In the case of Ireland, many of the BrowerStack employees have also gone back to their home-towns when we became a remote company. Remote work obviously helps in attracting the best talent because people can work from wherever they want to.

> **At BrowserStack, we have always invested in systems and processes that helped in open and transparent communication. We are good at documentation and sharing knowledge online with employees.**

Are we looking at a larger international presence in terms of our employee base? Not necessarily. One of the reasons is that compliance with local employment laws is an important factor when employing individuals in a new country. Let's say if I hire someone in a particular country, let's say in Europe, then dealing with the legal paperwork around employment in that country is a bit of a hassle; while one can have people or consultants manage it, the overall process will definitely involve more work for us, and hence is avoidable.

We instead focus on where we are, and getting the work done, rather than increasing our team's geographical footprint. Of course, there exists great talent in all countries, but I think for us this system works.

Q: What are your thoughts on BrowserStack's culture?

A: I suppose being in the tech business there are a few things that are really important to me from a company culture perspective. Everyone has to be honest and self-aware, which brings a sense of humility to the organisation.

Another given is that you have to be open and transparent, no politics, no BS, just be straight-shooters. So these are must-haves in any employee we hire, besides technical skills.

At BrowserStack, we have always invested in systems and processes that helped in open and transparent communication. We are good at documentation and sharing knowledge online with employees. This was particularly useful when we went fully remote during COVID-19. Operationally, we did not have issues in transitioning to a remote environment since everyone was fully comfortable with our online setup and using systems like Slack, Zoom, etc. The cultural challenge really comes while onboarding new employees in a remote working environment, especially freshers. How do you create the same experience of the office remotely? There is no personal interaction, water-cooler conversation, bonding over lunch or dinner, no weekend plans. This reduces the informal discussions that help in knowledge sharing and problem-solving. So as a company leadership, we've needed to double down and spend a lot of time communicating about the company culture and what is happening in different parts of BrowserStack. Earlier we didn't have to actively do this. We just did an open house once a quarter and people would attend. The rest would happen organically. Now you have to do a lot more communication from the top down to reinforce the culture.

Q: How do you personally define success?
A: For me, it's very simple. I think it's creating a big impact and continuing to work hard. If I am able to work hard, that's short-term success. Once you see the impact of the work on your customers, employees, and family, it gives you a sense of accomplishment and gratification. So, those are the two things that define success for me ∎

RAHUL **BAJAJ**

Who is **Rahul Bajaj?**

Rahul Bajaj was born on the 10th of June, 1938 in Kolkata, India to Savitri and Kamalnayan Bajaj. His grandfather, the Gandhian industrialist and freedom-fighter Jamnalal Bajaj, had established the Bajaj Group in 1926 with interests in cotton ginning, sugar, engineering, iron & steel, and electrical appliances. In 1948, the Bajaj Group had diversified into the import of 2 wheelers from Vespa and a decade later it received a license to manufacture 2 & 3 wheelers which it started doing under the name Bajaj Auto.

Rahul's parents were also staunch Gandhians and their values influenced his life and decisions. He studied at St. Stephen's College, the Government Law College, and went on to obtain his MBA from Harvard Business School in 1964, after which he returned to India and joined Bajaj Auto. Rahul was appointed as CEO of Bajaj Auto in 1968 and Managing Director in 1972 after his father passed away. He had to deal with the License Raj prevailing in the country at the time, constraining production and sales growth. Despite this, Rahul revolutionised Bajaj, launching well-priced scooters such as Chetak which was very popular with the Indian middle class. The iconic 'Hamara Bajaj' marketing campaign made Bajaj a household name in India. However, after the liberalisation of the early nineties, motorcyles became very popular and overtook scooter sales in 1999. Suddenly, Bajaj Auto faced tremendous competition from Japanese brands like Yamaha, Honda, and Suzuki, which had introduced motorcycles in partnership with other Indian companies. Bajaj was trailing them in the two-wheeler market and had to reinvent itself. This time Rahul Bajaj's son Rajiv took the lead and launched the Pulsar motorcycle whose affordability, engine, and design energized the younger audience. Rajiv Bajaj was appointed as Managing Director of Bajaj Auto Ltd in 2005.

Rahul Bajaj had also helped the Group to diversify. In 1987, Bajaj Auto Finance Ltd (BAFL) had been set up to finance the sale of Bajaj 2 & 3 wheelers. It has since evolved into a financial powerhouse called Bajaj FinServ which is India's most diversified non banking financial company. It is the most valuable asset of the Bajaj Group. This company is led by Rahul Bajaj's second son, Sanjiv Bajaj.

AWARDS AND RECOGNITION

- Rahul Bajaj was awarded India's third highest civilian award, the Padma Bhushan in 2001
- Appointed as a Knight in the Order of the Legion of Honour by the President of France in 2011
- Received the Ernst and Young (EY) Lifetime Achievement Award in 2004
- Conferred the Lifetime Achievement Award by The Economic Times in 2004
- Received the Alumni Achievement Award from the Harvard Business School in 2016
- Awarded CNBC-TV18 Outstanding Business Leader of the Year in 2014

KEY STRATEGIES AND SUCCESS FACTORS

Culture of Quality and Deploying Technology: Rahul Bajaj placed a lot of importance on building a culture of quality at Bajaj Auto. To achieve scale in the business and reduce production costs, he laid a strong emphasis on R&D and deployment of technology. He is best known for the Bajaj Chetak, an affordable and innovative scooter which took India by storm, selling 100,000 scooters per month in the 1990s. Bajaj Auto was late in entering the motorcycle business and ceded ground to Honda, Suzuki, and Yamaha. Despite the delayed entry into the motorcycle segment, Bajaj Auto developed its iconic model Pulsar in collaboration with Tokyo R&D Centre, and later with motorcycle designer Glynn Kerr. The Pulsar's affordability, engine variety and design, helped put Bajaj Auto in the forefront of the motorcycles segment.

Focus on Core Competence: He focused on Bajaj Auto's core competence which helped the company both from a valuation and reputation perspective. From early on, Rahul Bajaj was wary of debt and thus did not diversify too widely, as other business families often did. Generally averse to diversification, the only exception he made was in the areas of financial services, and general & life insurance. The diversification into financial services and insurance has been very successful and generated tremendous value for all stakeholders.

Ethics and Corporate Governance: Rahul Bajaj inherited Gandhian values from his family and these values were inculcated in Bajaj Auto as well. He was a key believer in good corporate governance and ethical behaviour. He used to say, "Ensuring that the consumer obtains the best possible product at the lowest possible price, and the employee gets a fair wage for a day's work, is the criterion of ethics in business." He had put in place a 'no bribe' rule at Bajaj Auto. No matter how pressing the circumstances, he refused to pay bribes. He was forthright and never hesitated to criticize a government policy if he thought that it was harmful.

ADITYA & KUMAR MANGALAM **BIRLA**

Who are **Aditya Vikram & Kumar Mangalam Birla?**

Aditya Vikram and Kumar Mangalam Birla are a testament to the heights that can be reached by a family business. Aditya Birla (grandson of GD Birla, the legendary industrialist and Gandhian) was born to Basant Kumar and Sarala Birla on 14th November, 1943 in Kolkata. After attending St. Xavier's College in Kolkata, he earned a degree in chemical engineering from MIT, Boston.

After returning to India in 1965, Aditya Birla set up Eastern Spinning Mills in Kolkata. The following year, he took over Indian Rayon, a sick viscose rayon yarn and fabric company. His father and grandfather were initially against this move, but Aditya persisted and successfully turned the company around. India was in the throes of the License Raj and Aditya felt that there were more opportunities to grow overseas. He expanded vigorously in Thailand, Malaysia, and Indonesia. By 1994, he was Thailand's largest exporter of synthetic yarn, Asia's largest producer of acrylic fibre, and the world's largest producer of rayon fibre. In Malaysia, Aditya's Pan Century Edible Oils was the world's largest single-location palm oil refinery. GD Birla passed away in 1983 bequeathing several major companies including Grasim and Hindalco to Aditya. Unfortunately, he too passed away when he was only 51, but during his short life Aditya successfully changed the Birla Group from being India focused to becoming a global conglomerate.

After Aditya Birla's passing, it was his son Kumar Mangalam who assumed Chairmanship of the Group in 1995 at the young age of 28. Kumar Mangalam was born on 14th June, 1967 in Kolkata. He obtained a bachelor's degree in commerce from Sydenham College, Mumbai and is also a Chartered Accountant. He pursued his MBA at London Business School. While there was some skepticism about Kumar Mangalam's ability to lead such a complex business group at a young age, he proved his skeptics wrong.

Under his leadership the Aditya Birla Group has acquired Indian Aluminium (INDAL) in 2000, copper mines in Australia, and L&T's Cement business. In 2007, Group company Hindalco acquired US based Novelis Inc, the world's leading manufacturer of aluminium rolled products. Aditya Birla Nuvo Ltd acquired Pantaloon Retail Ltd, from the Future Group in 2012. Group company UltraTech Cement is the largest manufacturer of grey cement, ready mix concrete (RMC) and white cement in India.

The Group's telecom company Idea Cellular was merged with Vodafone India, establishing Vodafone Idea. Aditya Birla Capital Ltd is the holding company for the Group's financial services business.

Since Kumar Mangalam Birla took over as Chairman in 1995, the Group's revenues have grown from US$ 2 billion to US$ 65 billion.

Forbes estimates Kumar Mangalam Birla's net worth to be US$ 19.7 billion.

KEY STRATEGIES AND SUCCESS FACTORS

Global Footprint: In the 1960s, Aditya Birla decided that he would expand his businesses in South-East Asia to avoid the constraints of the License Raj. He set up 19 companies outside India in Thailand, Malaysia, Indonesia, the Philippines and Egypt. By doing so, he set the Group on a roadmap for global growth. After Kumar Mangalam became Chairman of the Group, he successfully built on this vision. Today, the Aditya Birla Group operates in 36 countries and generates half its global revenues of US$ 65 billion from its overseas operations.

Inorganic Growth: Aditya Birla made his first acquisition in 1966 when he bought Indian Rayon from Morarjee Vaidya. After taking over as Chairman in 1995, Kumar Mangalam has used acquisitions to enter new markets and enhance its product portfolio by adding high value and high margin products. He has driven 40 successful acquisitions both in India and overseas, the highest by any Indian multinational.

AWARDS AND RECOGNITION

Aditya Vikram Birla
- Conferred Businessman of the Year Award by Business India in 1990
- Received Management Man of the Year Award from Bombay Management Association in 1992
- Conferred Lifetime Achievement Award posthumously by the All India Association of Industries in 1996

Kumar Mangalam Birla
- Conferred India's third highest civilian award, the Padma Bhushan in 2023
- Received Global Entrepreneur of The Year Award from The Indus Entrepreneurs (TiE) in 2021
- Named CNBC-TV18 – IBLA 'Outstanding Businessman of the Year' in 2017
- Conferred Global Leadership Award by US-India Business Council (USIBC) in 2014
- Received Business Leader of the Year Award from The Economic Times in 2013
- Conferred Global Business Leader Award by NASSCOM in 2012

GD **BIRLA**

Who is **GD Birla?**

GD Birla was born on 10th April, 1894 in Pilani, Rajasthan. His formal education ended at age 11 and he joined his father Raja Baldeo Das Birla's trading business. At the age of 16, he moved to Kolkata to set up up a jute trading business.

As a jute trader, he experienced first-hand the racist practices of the British while recognizing their strong business methods. He was keen to transition from being a trader to an industrialist and set up his first jute mill, Birla Jute Manufacturing Co Ltd against all odds. British and Scottish businesses tried to shut his business down by influencing certain banks not to give him loans. World War I had also begun, and exchange rates were awry making the import of machinery from Britain expensive. But he persevered and then went on to enter the cotton textile industry. In the 1930s, he diversified into the sugar and paper industries and in 1942 set up Hindustan Motors, India's first automobile factory. During the Quit India movement, he conceived the idea of setting up a bank using Indian capital and management. United Commercial Bank (Uco Bank) was established in Kolkata in 1943. He continued to grow from strength-to-strength post-independence when he invested in erstwhile European companies in tea, textiles, and other industries.

GD Birla was known to be a nationalist businessman who supported the Indian freedom struggle. He was close to Mahatma Gandhi and other leaders of the Indian National Congress and helped fund and establish several of Gandhiji's programs to help marginalised communities.

In the early 1920s, he created the Indian Chamber of Commerce to promote the cause of Indian businesses and in 1926 helped establish the Federation of Indian Chambers of Commerce & Industry (FICCI) which expressed support for India's freedom movement. In 1944, GD Birla along with other industrialists like JRD Tata and Purushottamdas Thakurdas helped formulate the 'Bombay Plan' a 15-year economic plan for India.

AWARDS AND RECOGNITION

- GD Birla awarded India's second highest civilian honour, Padma Vibhushan in 1957
- He represented India along with Gandhiji at the First and Second Round Table Conferences with the British between 1930 and 1931

KEY STRATEGIES AND SUCCESS FACTORS

Focus on the Greater Good: GD Birla was a philanthropist, nationalist and institution builder. He strongly supported Indian enterprises and established organizations such as FICCI and ICC to help advocate for them. He was a pioneer in education and founded the Birla Engineering College (renamed Birla Institute of Technology and Science in 1964), in Pilani. GD Birla helped set up schools, colleges, hospitals, temples and planetariums across India.

Foresight and Risk Taking: GD Birla was endowed with tremendous foresight and the ability to take calculated risks. Despite opposition from the British, he started his own jute mill in Kolkata. When World War I began, there was a huge demand for jute gunny bags and GD Birla profited greatly. Similarly, after Independence, GD Birla knew India would face a shortage of cotton for clothing, and decided to fill this gap with synthetic fibres. He established Hindalco in 1958 to indigenously meet the demand for aluminium.

Diversification: GD Birla's success at diversifying the Birla Group in a highly regulated economy is commendable. After India's Independence, he strategically acquired erstwhile European companies in textiles, tea, chemicals, rayon, and several other sectors. This helped build the Birla Group into a diversified conglomerate.

RADHAKISHAN **DAMANI**

Who is **Radhakishan Damani?**

Radhakishan Damani was born on 12th July, 1954 in Bikaner, Rajasthan. Coming from a humble background, Damani grew up in a one room apartment in Mumbai. He pursued a degree in commerce at the University of Mumbai but dropped out after one year. He set up an auto-ancillary business dealing in ball bearings but at the age of 32 he lost his father, and he shut down this business to enter the world of stock market investing. He set up an investment company called Bright Star in 1989 and became a SEBI registered stockbroker in 1992.

Damani was initially a trader, taking short-selling positions against the controversial investor Harshad Mehta who was artificially pumping up the value of stocks. In 1992, the stock market scam perpetrated by Harshad Mehta came to light, and prices of Mehta's stocks plummeted. Damani made a fortune from this turn of events. He then pivoted to value investment, identifying fundamentally strong stocks when they are undervalued and patiently waiting for them to appreciate. He bought stocks in high quality MNC companies such as Colgate, HUL, and Nestle that were available at a reasonable price. Over time, these MNC stocks appreciated tremendously creating significant wealth for Damani.

In 1999, Damani pivoted to the nascent organized retail business, taking up a franchise for the grocery co-operative chain Apna Bazar in Navi Mumbai, along with Damodar Mall. He was not convinced about Apna Bazar's business model, but spent his time learning about the business and developing relationships. He went on to found Avenue Supermarts Ltd in the year 2000 setting up a supermarket chain under the brand 'DMart'. Starting with one store in the Mumbai suburb of Powai, DMart today operates 338 stores across 10 states, 1 Union Territory and the National Capital Region. DMart's focus is to make available those products that are required daily by Indian families, at the best possible value.

Avenue Supermarts had a successful IPO in March 2017. The company is profitable and has been a significant value creator for investors.

Damani has also been making large real estate investments. In February 2023, Damani and his family concluded the largest real estate deal in India buying 28 luxury apartments in Mumbai in a single transaction.

Forbes estimates Radhakishan Damani's net worth to be US$ 16.6 billion.

KEY STRATEGIES AND SUCCESS FACTORS

Customer Centricity: Damani established DMart to meet the needs of the quintessential Indian middle class family. Located in middle-income residential areas, away from malls, DMart is relentlessly focused on providing value for the consumer's money. The chain's store managers are mandated to minimize operating costs and offer the lowest price in that area to ensure that the customers keep coming back. DMart's strong liquidity position allows it to pay suppliers upfront and enjoy significant cash discounts, which it passes on to consumers, resulting in loyalty and sales growth.

Long Term Focus: Damani's success in the stock market can be credited to his focus on value investing for the long term. He has invested in companies that had a strong foundation, sustainable business model, and enjoyed a competitive advantage in the marketplace. Through his patience and long-term vision, Damani has remained invested in such companies even if the market perception was negative in short term.

Prioritizing Profitability over Scale: In organised retail, it is common to lease stores so that new stores can be rapidly opened. This results in thin retail margins being squeezed even further, sometimes resulting in losses. Instead, Damani focused on buying the property where DMart stores were to be located. By doing so, DMart is able to deliver higher EBITDA margins since rental savings went straight to the company's bottom line. Damani was okay with DMart's slower rate of expansion and has always focused the business model on profitability over scale.

ADI GODREJ

Who is **Adi Godrej?**

Adi Godrej was born on 3rd April, 1942 into the Godrej business family in Mumbai. At 17, Adi Godrej went to study engineering at the Massachusetts Institute of Technology (MIT), Boston. However, he ended up pursuing a degree in business and graduated in 1963 with a M.Sc degree in management. He then returned to India to join his family's business that was involved in the manufacture of locks, safes, wardrobes, and soaps. At the time of his joining the company in 1963, its turnover was only INR 100 million and it was facing financial difficulties.

There were high expectations from Adi Godrej, since he was the only business graduate in the company at that time. He introduced process management techniques and was instrumental in systematising and modernising the outdated management structure and processes of the Group. He created a conducive environment in which qualified professionals could thrive and grow.

At the time of India's economic liberalization in 1991, many of the country's companies were fearful of MNCs. However, Adi Godrej established partnerships and joint ventures with large MNCs such as Procter & Gamble and General Electric (GE) which helped make the Godrej Group more efficient and competitive. He drove the global expansion and diversification of the Godrej Group while simultaneously ensuring that it stayed true to its credo of being 'Good and Green'.

In 2021, Adi Godrej stepped down as Chairman of Godrej Industries Ltd, the Group's flagship company. During his long and distinguished tenure, the Group's revenue grew by a compounded annual growth rate of 17 percent to US$ 5 billion. He is now Chairman Emeritus of Godrej Industries Ltd.

Forbes estimates Adi Godrej's net worth to be US$ 3.4 billion.

AWARDS AND RECOGNITION

- Adi Godrej was conferred India's third highest civilian award, the Padma Bhushan in 2013.
- Received the Leadership in Philanthropy Award in 2010
- Was named the Ernst & Young (EY) Entrepreneur of the Year in 2012
- Received the Asian Awards Entrepreneur of the Year in 2013
- Was adjudged the Business Leader of the Year by the All India Management Association in 2015
- Received the Golden Peacock Lifetime Achievement Award for Ethical Leadership in 2016
- Was named the Entrepreneur of the Year at the Asia Pacific Entrepreneurship Awards in 2010
- Received Chemexcil's Lifetime Achievement Award in 2010

KEY STRATEGIES AND
SUCCESS FACTORS

Professionalizing Management: When Adi Godrej joined the Godrej Group upon his return from MIT, he restructured the company to upgrade management processes by incorporating concepts like human resources, accounting, and cost-optimisation. He also hired management graduates to create a goal-oriented culture. This has resulted in the Godrej Group being run as a very professional organisation

Globalization: Adi Godrej focused on expanding the Godrej Group into global markets. One of its group companies, Godrej Consumer Products Ltd (GCPL) has a '3 by 3' approach to international expansion whereby it builds its presence in '3' emerging markets (Asia, Africa, and Latin America) across '3' categories (home care, personal wash, and hair care products). The company has a leadership position in most categories in the domestic and international markets. Today, the Godrej Group exports products to over 80 countries.

Innovation: In the early 1990s, many companies viewed the Government's liberalization policies and opening up of the economy as a threat to their survival due to the higher competitiveness of MNCs. Adi Godrej did not agree with this viewpoint. Under his leadership, the Godrej Group focused on innovation, embracing technology for product development and operations.
Decades later, when the pandemic struck in 2020, being technology-savvy paved the way for the Godrej Group's digitisation and growth through e-commerce.

HARSH **GOENKA**

Who is **Harsh Goenka?**

Harsh Goenka was born on 10th December, 1957 in Kolkata, into a renowned business family. The Goenka business was founded early in the 19th century and Harsh is a fifth-generation entrepreneur. Harsh's father Dr. Rama Prasad Goenka, a successful industrialist, established RPG Enterprises, an industrial conglomerate in 1979.

Harsh graduated with a degree in economics from St. Xavier's College in Kolkata, later pursuing an MBA from IMD, Switzerland. He then returned to Mumbai and worked briefly at a textile company before being appointed as Managing Director of CEAT Ltd in 1983. He became Chairman of the RPG Enterprises in 1990, succeeding his father. RPG Enterprises has grown inorganically and Harsh was involved in all its acquisitions - CEAT Ltd, KEC Ltd, Searle (now RPG Life Sciences), HMV, CESC, Harrisons Malayalam, Spencers and ICIM (now Zensar).

In 2010, Dr. Rama Prasad Goenka divided RPG Enterprises between Harsh and his brother Sanjiv Goenka (also featured in this publication). At the time, the revenue of the undivided RPG Group was US\$ 2.86 billion. Harsh received the following companies as part of this amicable split: CEAT Ltd, KEC Ltd, RPG Life Sciences and Zensar. Today, the revenue of only Harsh Goenka's companies is US\$ 4.4 billion, and the market capitalization of the Group has grown several times.

Harsh has been a key proponent of corporate social responsibility (CSR): RPG Foundation (the Group's public charitable trust) is very active in eye care, women's empowerment, education, and local community development.

Harsh is also an avid collector of contemporary art.

Forbes estimates Harsh Goenka's net worth to be US\$ 3.2 billion.

AWARDS AND RECOGNITION

- Harsh Goenka received the Navbharat Times Award for Corporate Leadership and Contribution to Society in 2023
- Received the Business Leader of the Year award at the Hello! Hall of Fame Awards in 2017

KEY STRATEGIES AND SUCCESS FACTORS

Operating Excellence: Harsh Goenka places a lot of emphasis in operating excellence at RPG Enterprises. This involves setting in place systems and structures that support the Group's objectives and help streamline the operations of the conglomerate. Such measures include handpicking executives for each company, defining clear objectives, and reviewing progress. In fact, according to many senior executives who have worked with him, Harsh is the 'master of reviews', taking stock of results, updates and performance.

People-First Culture: A large part of Harsh Goenka's success stems from the People-First culture at RPG Enterprises which is reflected in its motto, 'Hello Happiness'. The Group's vision statement is, "Unleash Talent, Touch Lives, Outperform and Be Happy". This approach starts at the top, with Harsh taking a keen interest in driving people practices and culture at RPG Enterprises. He has also sought to create an informal, first-name environment at RPG Enterprises.

Mergers and Acquisitions: In the 1980s, Harsh Goenka and his father Dr. Rama Prasad Goenka utilised mergers and acquisitions to their advantage. At the time, India was a controlled economy and achieving inorganic growth was both difficult and dangerous. They acquired CEAT Ltd, KEC International, Searle (now RPG Life Sciences), ICIM (now Zensar) and several other companies. RPG Enterprises also entered into Joint Ventures (JVs) to drive growth, and at one point it had JVs with 13 Fortune 500 companies.

SANJIV GOENKA

Who is **Sanjiv Goenka?**

Sanjiv Goenka was born on the 29th of January, 1961 in Kolkata into a renowned business family. The Goenka business was founded early in the 19th century and Sanjiv is a fifth-generation entrepreneur. He was the second son of Dr. Rama Prasad Goenka, a successful industrialist, who established RPG Enterprises, an industrial conglomerate in 1979. His elder brother is Harsh Goenka, who is also featured in this book.

Sanjiv graduated with a Bachelor's Degree in Commerce from St. Xavier's College, Kolkata and joined the family business. His first assignment was at Deccan Fibre in Hyderabad, a company that manufactured fiberglass. Next, he was appointed as Deputy Managing Director of Dunlop, at the age of 23. In 1989, at the young age of 28, Sanjiv acquired Calcutta Electric Supply Corporation (CESC), despite the disapproval of his father. Kolkata had been facing daily power-cuts caused by demand-supply mismatch, low productivity at CESC, and T&D losses. Sanjiv augmented electricity supply by setting up new power plants, drove efficiency, and turned the company around.

Dr. Rama Prasad Goenka had grown RPG Enterprises acquiring companies like CEAT Ltd, KEC Ltd, Searle, HMV, Harrisons Malayalam, and ICIM (now Zensar). In 2010, Dr. Rama Prasad Goenka divided RPG Enterprises between Sanjiv and Harsh Goenka. At the time, the revenue of the undivided RPG Group was US$ 2.86 billion. Sanjiv inherited CESC, Phillips Carbon Black, Spencers Retail, and Saregama (formerly HMV) and established the RP-Sanjiv Goenka Group. He expanded the Group's activities into several areas:

- ITeS: RP-Sanjiv Goenka Group acquired FirstSource Solutions Ltd
- Media & Entertainment: Besides growing Saregama, Sanjiv acquired assets like Open and Fortune India magazines, and Editorji, a digital newspaper
- Consumer and Retail: In addition to Spencers, the Group acquired the Nature's Basket retail chain from Godrej. In the foods business, it set up Too Yumm!, a low calorie snacking brand, and acquired Apricot Foods Ltd, a packaged foods company. It also entered the Ayurvedic medicines and products category by picking up a majority in Dr. Vaidya's brand. It entered luxury retail by setting up Quest Mall in Kolkata.
- Sports: The Group entered the sports business in 2014 and owns the cricket franchises Lucknow Super Giants and Durban's Super Giants, and the football franchise Mohan Bagan Super Giants.
- Education & Infrastructure: Some institutions controlled by the RP-Sanjiv Goenka group are the Woodlands Hospital, International Management Institute (IMI) and the RP Goenka International School.

Before the split of RPG Enterprises, its combined total revenue was US$ 2.86 billion. Today, RP-Sanjiv Goenka Group's revenues alone stand at US$ 4.3 billion; its asset base is over US$ 7 billion.

Forbes estimates Sanjiv Goenka's net worth to be US$ 3.6 billion.

KEY STRATEGIES AND **SUCCESS FACTORS**

Revenue Diversification: Sanjiv Goenka has been successful in diversifying the Group's revenue streams. The Group used to get 80% of its revenues from the regulated power sector. Through the turnaround and growth of other businesses such as Consumer & Retail, the Group's revenues are now evenly matched between power and the other businesses.

Focus on Operational Efficiency and Profitability: To realize his vision for the Group, Sanjiv knew that he would need to enhance operational efficiency and turn around its loss making entities. He took steps to make the carbon black, music and film content, and ITeS businesses profitable, changing management teams where necessary. His clear message to the management teams was that the businesses needed to be profitable, not just generate top-line growth. The Group's flagship company CESC also had businesses like retail and real estate, the value of which needed to be unlocked. To achieve this goal, he split CESC into three parts in 2018 — power generation and distribution business, retail business, and CESC Ventures, which included IT and FMCG. Value was unlocked by listing CESC Ventures and Spencer's Retail on the bourses.

AWARDS AND RECOGNITION

- Sanjiv Goenka was conferred Banga Bhibhushan, the highest civilian award in West Bengal in 2015
- Received the Asian Leadership Award from Asian Association of Management Organisations In 2019
- Conferred the Legacy Honor by the Young Presidents Organization (YPO) in 2002
- Received the Indian Business Leader of the Year Award at the Global India Business Meeting held in 2013

YUSUF **HAMIED**

Who is **Yusuf Hamied?**

Yusuf Hamied was born on 25th July, 1936 in Lithuania. Inspired by Mahatma Gandhi, his father Dr. KA Hamied founded Cipla, a pharmaceutical company in 1935. Yusuf grew up in Mumbai and then attended Cambridge where he received a BA in Chemistry in 1957, followed by a Ph.D, just before he turned 24.

In 1960, Yusuf joined Cipla as R&D officer. He observed that India followed colonial-era patent laws which favoured MNCs and were very restrictive for Indian Pharma companies. In 1961, along with a few like-minded businessmen, he set up the Indian Drug Manufacturers Association (IDMA) which successfully persuaded the government to abolish product patents in 1972, freeing up the production of key drugs for Indian pharma companies. This enabled India to become a producer of pharmaceuticals for the world. Yusuf guided Cipla into the manufacture of active pharmaceutical ingredients (APIs) in 1961, making the company self sufficient in end-to-end drug manufacturing.

He has led the development of multi-drug combination pills for diseases such as TB that affect developing countries. Yusuf's greatest moment came in 2001 when he took on pharma MNCs to offer a fixed dose combination Triomune for the treatment of the HIV/ AIDS epidemic which was ravaging the world. Thanks to him, Pharma MNCs were also forced to cut prices, saving lives around the world.

Under Yusuf's leadership, Cipla became the third-largest generic drug company in India. He now serves as Cipla's Non-Executive Chairman.

Forbes estimates Yusuf Hamied's net worth to be US$ 2.8 billion.

AWARDS AND RECOGNITION

- Yusuf Hamied received India's third highest civilian award, Padma Bhushan in 2005
- He was given an honorary doctorate in science by Cambridge in 2014, the highest honour the University can bestow
- Was named a Fellow of the Christ's College, Cambridge, UK in 2004
- The Cambridge Department of Chemistry was named after him in 2020
- Was named an honorary fellow of the Royal Society of Chemistry in 2012
- Was named honorary fellow of the Indian National Science Academy
- Adjudged the CNN–IBN Person of the Year in Business in 2012
- Received the Sir PC Ray Award for the development of indigenous technology in 1983

KEY STRATEGIES AND
SUCCESS FACTORS

Focus on the Greater Good: Yusuf Hamied inherited his father's mindset of providing affordable drugs to poor citizens in India. He made affordable healthcare the focus of Cipla's efforts. His battle against Pharma MNCs by offering HIV/AIDS drugs at a fraction of MNC prices won him and Cipla global acclaim. The magazine India Today wrote, "the story of Yusuf Hamied will make every Indian proud as he was the only man who decided to walk against the tide and sell drugs to save lives without focusing on profits."

Incremental Innovation: Yusuf Hamied realized very early on that new drugs that were not produced by MNCs like Pfizer, did not find easy market acceptance. Thus, instead of developing new drugs, he made Cipla focus on 'incremental innovation' which meant improving existing formulae. It is this strategy that allowed Cipla to produce Triomune, a single drug to manage HIV/AIDS, instead of a cocktail of three drugs.

Learning and Knowledge: One of the primary reasons behind Yusuf Hamied's success is his personal quest for learning. His own knowledge and hands-on involvement enabled him to pioneer fixed drug combination (FDC) treatment for HIV/AIDS, TB, Asthma, etc.

RAKESH **JHUNJHUNWALA**

Who is **Rakesh Jhunjhunwala?**

Rakesh Jhunjhunwala was born on 5th July, 1960 in Mumbai. His father was an income tax officer and his mother a homemaker. He graduated from the Sydenham College of Commerce & Economics, Mumbai and then went on to become a Chartered Accountant.

His interest in the stock market stemmed from his father who guided him with market advice but did not give him any funds to invest. While at college, Rakesh invested his savings of INR 5,000 and began his journey in the stock market. His first large profit came from his investment in Tata Tea in 1986 and he made about INR 500,000 from the transaction. There was no looking back!

Right since the early days, Rakesh was an astute investor picking up stocks in companies such as Sesa Goa, Tata Tea, Praj Industries, Tata Power, etc, which he believed were undervalued. He placed one of his biggest bets in his early days just before the Union Budget of 1989; VP Singh was Prime Minister, the Finance Minister was a socialist and the markets had fallen because it was widely assumed that the Budget would not be pro-business. Rakesh took a contrarian position and aggressively purchased stocks because he believed that VP Singh's background would not let him disappoint the business community. His instinct proved right; the Union Budget was pro-business and in a few months, Rakesh had multiplied his net worth by 20 times, from INR 25 million to INR 500 million.

In 1992, he set up his asset management firm 'RARE Enterprises' and over the years invested in companies like Titan Company, STAR Health, Metro Brands, Tata Motors, CRISIL, Lupin, Fortis, Canara Bank, Indian Hotels, Federal Bank, Nazara Technologies, etc. His final large investment was in Akasa Air, India's newest airline in which he acquired an approximately 40% stake for US$ 35 million.

Fondly known as the Big Bull, Rakesh Jhunjhunwala's net worth was estimated to be US$ 5.8 billion when he passed away in August 2022.

AWARDS AND RECOGNITION

- Rakesh Jhunjhunwala was posthumously awarded India's fourth highest civilian honour, the Padma Shri in 2023
- Listed in the Edelgive Hurun India Philanthropy List 2021

KEY STRATEGIES AND
SUCCESS FACTORS

Size of the Addressable Market: Before investing, Rakesh Jhunjhunwala always focused on the size of the addressable market for a company's product or services. He believed that it is important to invest in companies that are growing rapidly in a market the size of which is also growing well. Growing markets provide a long growth runway for companies.

Invest in Companies that have a Competitive Advantage: Rakesh Jhunjhunwala always said that one should invest in companies and not their stocks, i.e., invest in companies that have competitive advantages over their peers.This competitive advantage could be in the form of brand, capital or technology.

Corporate Governance: One of Rakesh Jhunjhunwala's key investment criteria before investing in a company was its level of corporate governance. If a company's management had poor integrity, he would not invest in it. He liked to place his bets on hardworking and honest teams that were frugal in their approach. The high level of integrity in Tata Group companies was one of the reasons that he invested in so many of them.

SAJJAN **JINDAL**

Who is **Sajjan Jindal?**

Sajjan Jindal was born on the 5th of December, 1959 to Om Prakash Jindal and Savitri Devi Jindal. Sajjan's father OP Jindal set up a steel pipe manufacturing unit in 1964 which grew into a successful steel giant.

Sajjan graduated from the MS Ramaiah Institute of Technology in 1982 with a bachelors degree in mechanical engineering. Thereafter, he joined the family business and was entrusted with the responsibility of turning around OP Jindal Group's fledgling steel facility located near Mumbai. In 1989, he promoted Jindal Iron and Steel Company Ltd (JISCO) to produce cold rolled and galvanised steel sheet products. His next leap in the steel industry came when he set up a large-scale steel integrated plant at Vijayanagar in Karnataka, promoted by him as Jindal Vijayanagar Steel Ltd. This is the largest single-location steel-producing facility in India.

He promoted JSW Energy Limited (JSWEL), Jindal Praxair Oxygen Limited (JPOCL) and Vijayanagar Minerals Private Limited (VMPL) to ensure complete integration of the manufacturing process. In 2005, Sajjan made the strategic decision to merge JISCO and JVSL under JSW Steel to reduce administrative costs, optimize tax planning, and improve the balance sheet. Today, JSW Steel is India's largest steel producer, and is further expanding its production capacity to 37 million tonnes per annum (MTPA) by FY 2025, and then to 50 MTPA by the end of the decade.

Under Sajjan's leadership, JSW has also expanded into other core sectors of the economy including power, cement, and paints. It has recently forayed into the automotive industry by collaborating with SAIC Motor to acquire a 35% stake in MG Motor India.

JSW Sports, the sports arm of the JSW Group, was established in 2012 to play a leading role in creating a sporting culture in India by maximising the potential of Indian sports and athletes. Today, JSW Sports is associated with champion teams like Bengaluru FC, Delhi Capitals, Haryana Steelers, Pretoria Capitals, and Delhi Capitals Women's Team and champion athletes like Neeraj Chopra, Axar Patel, Dhruv Jurel, Sakshi Malik, Jemimah Rodrigues, and Shafali Verma.

JSW Group is a key constituent of the OP Jindal Group, the Chairperson of which is Savitri Devi Jindal (Sajjan Jindal's mother).

Forbes estimates Savitri Devi Jindal and family's net worth to be US$ 29.8 billion.

KEY STRATEGIES AND **SUCCESS FACTORS**

Taking Technological Risks: Sajjan Jindal has always taken technological risks to build state-of-the-art steel manufacturing facilities. For example, he bet on the new Corex technology while building the Vijayanagar steel plant. He persevered despite initial technology challenges to build India's largest integrated steel manufacturing facility.

Inorganic Growth: Sajjan Jindal has deployed inorganic growth as key growth strategy. The Group continues to explore strategic acquisitions to drive growth, both in India and overseas. The strategic joint venture with SAIC Motor whereby JSW Group acquired 35% in MG Motor India is the most recent example of its inorganic growth.

Diversification: Sajjan Jindal has leveraged diversification opportunities to grow the Group. In recent years, diversification has become a core driver to meet Sajjan's goal of increasing the Group's revenue by 3-4 times to US$ 60-80 billion by 2030. JSW has taken major steps in power, ports, paint, cement, and automobiles. The Group has also strategically diversified into renewable energy, given India's green energy aspirations.

AWARDS AND RECOGNITION

- Sajjan Jindal received the Ernst & Young (EY) Entrepreneur of the Year Award for India in 2022
- Was elected as the first Indian Chairman of the World Steel Association
- Received the Willy Korf/Ken Iverson Steel Vision Award in 2009
- Awarded CEO of the Year by Business Standard in 2018
- Conferred Best CEO Award by Business Today Magazine in 2019
- Received 'National Metallurgist Award: Industry' instituted by the Ministry of Steel, Government of India in 2014
- Conferred the IIM-JRD Tata Award for Excellence in Corporate Leadership in the Metallurgical industry in 2017

NITHIN & NIKHIL KAMATH

Who are **Nithin & Nikhil Kamath?**

Nithin and Nikhil Kamath were born on 5th October, 1979 and 5th September, 1986 respectively in Shivamogga, Karanataka. Their father was employed with Canara Bank while their mother was a homemaker. According to interviews given by the brothers, neither of them were academically inclined but were more entrepreneurial in nature. Nithin dropped out his computer engineering program while Nikhil dropped out of school in the tenth grade.

Nithin began managing his father's equity trading account when he was 17 and still a student. He gained valuable trading experience at that time and was doing well until the dotcom bust of the early 2000s. Facing losses and unpaid loans, he was also employed at a call centre. A chance meeting with a non-resident Indian named Prakash in a gym changed his life. Prakash gave him INR 2.5 million to invest and also introduced other clients to Nithin. Soon Nithin was managing money for multiple people. He found that logging into multiple broking accounts to execute transactions was not easy. He therefore decided to become a sub-broker for Reliance Money, setting up Investments Unlimited which became Kamath Associates when Nikhil joined him after a few months. In working with various brokers, Nithin and Nikhil found that they were expensive, opaque and inaccessible.

In 2008, they became members of the National Stock Exchange (NSE) allowing them to trade on NSE's NOW platform that was offered free to brokers. It led Nithin and Nikhil to question whether by leveraging technology, they could they disrupt pricing in the broking business. On August 15th, 2010 they launched Zerodha, becoming pioneers of the discount broking business in India. Their objective was to break all barriers faced by traders and investors in India viz., cost, customer support, and technology. Zerodha's innovative pricing models such as flat fee trades, combined with its technology, has reshaped the stockbroking landscape in India.

Zerodha has nearly 6.5 million active users currently. Fully bootstrapped, Zerodha is a privately held company. It's revenue for FY23 was over US$ 820 million and its profit after tax was US$ 350 million. It is India's most profitable brokerage by far. Nithin and Nikhil Kamath's fintech fund and incubator Rainmatter has invested in several fintech startups with the goal of growing the Indian capital market.

Forbes estimates the net worth of Nithin & Nikhil Kamath and family to be US$ 5.5 billion.

AWARDS AND RECOGNITION

- Nithin Kamath received the Entrepreneur of the Year award at The Economic Times Awards for Corporate Excellence in 2023
- Zerodha received The Economic Times Start-up of the year (bootstrapped) Award in 2016
- Nithin Kamath was awarded Emerging Entrepreneur of the Year by CII in 2014

KEY STRATEGIES AND **SUCCESS FACTORS**

Disruptive Pricing and Low-Cost Structure: Zerodha completely disrupted the pricing model for broking firms in India. With minimum registration fees and flat trading fees, they took the market by storm. Zerodha's online model and low-cost structure has enabled it to keep pricing to the bare minimum, and yet remain very profitable.

Effective Use of Technology: Nithin and Nikhil Kamath were inspired by their experience using the NSE NOW platform that allowed brokers to trade free on the platform thanks to the effectively deployment of technology. Consequently, they bet big on technology and Zerodha's Kite trading platform and its central dashboard Console are extremely popular amongst users.

Zerodha has also launched Kite Connect APIs to enable startups to build innovative trading and investment platforms.

The Power of Bootstrapping: By bootstrapping Zerodha, Nithin and Nikhil Kamath were able to avoid onboarding external investors such as VC and PE firms whose processes tend to be bureaucratic. This has enabled Zerodha to stay nimble and agile, and make decisions quickly, so that it evolves faster than competition. In a company with multiple investors, or in a financial institution, decision-making is generally much slower.

UDAY **KOTAK**

Who is **Uday Kotak?**

Uday Kotak was born on 15th March, 1959 in Mumbai into a family that was involved in the commodities trade. His father had moved to Mumbai from Karachi during Partition and he grew up in a large joint family. Growing up, Uday was passionate about cricket, mathematics, and playing the sitar.

After graduating from Sydenham College, he went on to complete his MBA in 1982 from JBIMS. Uday was not keen on joining the family business as 14 family members already worked there; he also received a job offer from Hindustan Unilever Ltd. However, encouraged by his father who gave him 300 square feet in the family's office, Uday decided to set up his own finance business.

He raised seed capital of US$ 80,000 from family and friends and set up Kotak Capital Management Finance Ltd in 1985 which was engaged in the bill discounting business. Anand Mahindra of the Mahindra family also invested in the business and the company was renamed Kotak Mahindra Finance Ltd (KMFL) in 1986. The company entered into the lease and hire purchase business in 1987 and then diversified into auto finance in 1990. The Investment Banking division was established in 1991.

The next diversification was into Mutual Funds with the establishment of Kotak Mahindra AMC in 1998. Uday then led the company into insurance in 2001 setting up a JV with Old Mutual plc.

Under Uday's leadership, Kotak Mahindra was the first non-banking finance company (NBFC) in India to receive a commercial banking licence in 2003.

The next expansion was into private equity in 2004. Kotak then launched a pension fund in 2009 under the National Pension Scheme.

In 2014, Kotak acquired a 15% stake in Multi Commodity Exchange of India Ltd (MCX). In the following year, ING Vysya Bank was merged into Kotak Mahindra Bank; Kotak Mahindra General Insurance also received IRDAI approval to commence the general insurance business.

Today, the Kotak Mahindra Group is a financial behemoth with a strong presence across the Banking, Financial Services and Insurance (BFSI) landscape.

Forbes estimates Uday Kotak's net worth to be US$ 13.6 billion.

AWARDS AND RECOGNITION

- Awarded 'Best CEO in Banking Sector' at the Business Today Best CEO Awards in 2019
- Received The Economic Times Business Leader of the Year Award in 2015
- Received the Ernst & Young (EY) World Entrepreneur Award in 2014

KEY STRATEGIES AND **SUCCESS FACTORS**

Institution Builder: Uday Kotak has built very credible institutions based on integrity, rather than taking shortcuts for growth. Consequently, he is highly respected in the financial and banking community, and by the Government. Because of his stature, Uday Kotak was brought in by the Government to become Chairman of the troubled IL&FS in 2018 and held this position till April 2023. During his tenure as Chairman of IL&FS, the institution was able to successfully address nearly US$ 6.8 billion of its outstanding debt.

Sound Risk Management: Uday Kotak has always been very prudent in managing risks by focusing on risk-return assessment at the Kotak Mahindra Group, rather than being obsessed with size. His mantra is, "Return of capital is more important than return on capital."

Going Digital: Under his leadership, the Group was quick to innovate and leverage technology. For example, Kotak Mahindra Bank's 811 digital banking savings account can be opened online within 5 minutes from anywhere; it deploys a paperless, video-based Know Your Customers (KYC) process.

ARVIND **MAFATLAL**

Who is **Arvind Mafatlal?**

Arvind Mafatlal was born on 27th October, 1923 in Ahmedabad. In 1905, his grandfather, Mafatlal Gagalbhai had set up a textile mill in Ahmedabad, laying the foundation of the Mafatlal Group. Arvind Mafatlal was educated in Mumbai, graduating from St. Xavier's High School and then Sydenham College.

Mafatlal Group made rapid strides by investing in and modernizing cotton textile mills; it was the third-largest mill owner in India in 1954 when Arvind Mafatlal took over the leadership of the Group.

In line with Arvind Mafatlal's vision, the Group began diversifying into multiple industries like chemicals, plastics, engineering, finance and information technology, thus becoming one of the country's early conglomerates. Arvind Mafatlal set up several joint ventures with global giants such as Shell, Hoechst, and Monsanto.

Group entity NOCIL was incorporated in 1961 and is India's largest rubber chemicals manufacturer.

Founded by Arvind Mafatlal in 1967, Navin Fluorine International Ltd is one of the country's largest manufacturers of specialty fluorochemicals. Today, it is part of the Padmanabh Mafatlal Group.

Arvind Mafatlal played an important role in the post-Independence industrial growth of India. He was a deeply spiritual and ethical person who improved the lives of the downtrodden through various social initiatives.

AWARDS AND RECOGNITION

- Arvind Mafatlal was awarded the Durga Prasad Khaitan Memorial Gold Medal for Business in 1966
- Received the Sir Jehangir Ghandy Gold Medal for Industrial Peace from Xavier Labour Relations Institute, Jamshedpur in 1978
- Was bestowed with the Lions' Humanitarian Award by the International Association of Lions Clubs of the US in 1993.

KEY STRATEGIES AND
SUCCESS FACTORS

Diversification: Diversification was an important part of Arvind Mafatlal's strategy to convert a textile-focused business into a conglomerate. Rapid diversification into rubber chemicals, specialty chemicals and petrochemicals, allowed the Mafatlal Group to grow, simultaneously putting post-Independence India on the global industrial map.

Partnerships: Forging partnerships with global leaders was a key part of Arvind Mafatlal's strategy, especially to drive the group's diversification. Early partnerships with global leaders like Shell, Hoechst, and Monsanto, allowed the company to scale-up quickly and successfully.

Focus on the Greater Good: Arvind Mafatlal was a philanthropist who worked towards the greater good, focusing on social reforms, education, and agricultural development. He worked with Manibhai Bhimbhai Desai, an associate of Mahatma Gandhi, to set up the Bharatiya Agro Industries Foundation (BAIF). The organization creates opportunities for gainful self-employment of rural families, especially disadvantaged sections, ensuring sustainable livelihood, enriched environment, improved quality of life and good human values.

ANAND **MAHINDRA**

Who is **Anand Mahindra?**

Anand Mahindra was born on 1st March, 1955 in Mumbai. His father, Harish Mahindra was part of Mahindra Group which was active in manufacturing of tractors, utility vehicles, alloy steel, etc. He pursued a undergraduate degree in film-making from Harvard University and thereafter received an MBA from Harvard Business School in 1981.

Anand Mahindra began his career as executive assistant to the Financial Director of Mahindra Ugine Steel Company Ltd (MUSCO). In the early 1980s, suddenly there was excess capacity in the alloy steel sector and MUSCO was bleeding. He turned around the loss-making company by squeezing efficiencies from the supply chain and selling surplus inventory. He went on to become President & Deputy MD of MUSCO. He moved to Mahindra & Mahindra Ltd (M&M) as Deputy MD in 1991 and sought to improve productivity in the factory. This led to a massive strike and his office was surrounded by angry workers baying for his blood. Only 36 years old, Anand Mahindra held firm and the workers finally yielded, improving productivity by over 50%. There was no looking back.

Over the years, he served as Managing Director, Vice-Chairman, Executive Chairman and today is Chairman of the Mahindra Group which encompasses automobiles, tractors, farm machinery, finance, real estate, agri, hospitality, renewables, digital, and steel.

His audacious bet in developing the Scorpio automobile from scratch in 1997 has culminated in the Mahindra Group's strong position today in the SUV space through a wide range of models.

Anand Mahindra was a co-promoter of Kotak Mahindra Bank and continues to own a small stake in it.

Forbes estimates Anand Mahindra's net worth at US$ 2.7 billion.

AWARDS AND RECOGNITION

- Anand Mahindra received India's third highest civilian award, the Padma Bhushan in 2020
- Was appointed as a Knight of the Order of Merit by the President of the French Republic in 2004
- Featured in the Fortune Magazine's Top 50 Greatest Leaders list in 2014
- Was adjudged as the Person of the Year by Auto Monitor in 2005
- Received the CNBC Asia Business Leader Award in 2006
- Received the Inspiring Corporate Leader of the Year Award from NDTV Profit in 2007

KEY STRATEGIES AND SUCCESS FACTORS

Autonomy to Senior Management: Anand Mahindra restructured the system within the Mahindra Group to encourage successful expansion into different sectors. This restructuring created independent and empowered Presidents for each sector. This autonomy and freedom helped encourage higher growth and better performance.

Measured Risk Taking: Assessing and taking prudent risks is one of the most important tasks of a leader. Anand Mahindra has often said this in the context of the Jaguar Land Rover (JLR) acquisition which he did not pursue though it seemed attractive. After talking to several experts, he decided that if he paid the high price that JLR was demanding, an industry downturn could irreparably damage the Mahindra Group. His attitude is to take measured risks and walk away if they are too high.

Learning from Setbacks: Anand Mahindra believes that business setbacks are great opportunities to learn. In 1995, M&M and Ford Motors forged a partnership to manufacture the Ford Escort. While the venture failed, he said, "The 300 people who put the Ford Escort together were the first ones to work on the Scorpio. It can be argued that we would not have been able to make the Scorpio without the Ford joint venture."

KALANITHI **MARAN**

Who is **Kalanithi Maran?**

Kalanithi Maran was born on the 22nd of July 1964, in Chennai, Tamil Nadu into a political family. His father Murasoli Maran was a Member of Parliament and also Union Minister of Commerce. His grand- uncle M. Karunanidhi was the former Chief Minister of Tamil Nadu. He graduated from Loyola College in Chennai and subsequently obtained an MBA from the University of Scranton, Pennsylvania. While studying for his MBA, he was amazed at the wide variety of television channels available in the US.

After graduating, Kalanithi returned to India and worked in multiple roles in his family's modest publication business. In 1990, he started Poomalai, a monthly video news magazine recorded on VHS video cassettes. He ran the business for 2 years but had to shut it down due to proliferating piracy.

In April 1993, Maran started Sun TV, taking a bank loan of US$86,000 guaranteed by his father. He needed a slot on a transponder in order to telecast and reached out to Subhash Chandra who had recently who set up Zee TV. A junior editor at Zee rejected Kalanithi's proposal because he said that the size of the Tamil audience would not be sufficient. Kalanithi realized that everyone underestimated the potential of the South Indian audience. He managed to obtain a transponder slot from Asian Television Network (ATN) and commenced with 3 hours of Tamil language programming. Leveraging his video business connections, he convinced video shop owners to become cable operators and expanded his distribution network across the state. He quickly expanded to 24-hour channels spanning several languages: Tamil, Malayalam, Telugu, Kannada, and Bengali. In 1998, India liberalized satellite broadcast rules and Kalanithi was a major beneficiary, being one of the first persons to get a licence. Over the years, the Sun Group expanded into film, radio, and newspapers. Despite Sun TV's growth, in 2007, Kalanithi faced several challenges arising from a perceived rift with his uncle who was the Chief MInister. He maintained a low profile and worked his way through the crisis to regain dominance of the industry over time.

In 2010, Kalanathi invested in the aviation industry by acquiring a large stake in SpiceJet, and ran the airline for four years. Given the difficulty in the aviation sector, he divested his stake in SpiceJet in 2015. His continued success in the television industry has earned him the title, "The Television King of South India". He also owns the IPL cricket franchise 'Sunrisers Hyderabad'.

Forbes estimates Kalanithi Maran's net worth to be US$ 3.2 billion.

AWARDS AND RECOGNITION

- Kalanithi Maran received the Asia Innovator of the Year Award from CNBC in 2011
- Received Businessman of the Year Award from Economic Times in 2010
- Awarded Entrepreneur of the Year by TiE Con in 2009
- Received Entrepreneurship Award from CNBC in 2005
- Conferred Outstanding Businessman Award in Entertainment & Information Sector by Ernst & Young (EY) in 2004

KEY STRATEGIES AND
SUCCESS FACTORS

Identifying an Untapped Market: When Kalanathi Maran created Sun TV, he had the clear vision of tapping into the South Indian audience, both in the country and overseas. Despite accounting for a fourth of India's population and a third of Indians with TV sets in 1993, there were no TV channels catering to the South Indian audience. He catered to this unaddressed market by expanding Sun TV's distribution reach rapidly. By also targeting the South Indian diaspora, Sun TV has successfully expanded its reach to 27 countries.

Creating a Competitive Edge: Kalanathi created a competitive edge initially by adopting a 'private producer' model that charged producers a fixed fee to air their shows; the entire inventory risk was taken by the shows' producers and all advertising revenue would accrue to them. He also formed exclusive partnerships with producers, restricting them from associating with Sun's competitors; this gave him a dominant position in the market. Sun TV also retained the right to drop producers if their shows did not attract an audience. This helped maintain quality of content, enabling Sun TV to stay profitable and debt free in a capital intensive industry.

Harnessing Political Connections: Although the success of Kalanithi Maran can be mostly attributed to his own hard work and strategic thinking, he has also harnessed his political connections very effectively to help Sun TV reach a dominant position in South India.

HARSH MARIWALA

Who is **Harsh Mariwala?**

Harsh Mariwala was born in 1951 in Mumbai, India into a business family that traded in spices. In 1948, his father and uncles had founded Bombay Oil Mills which manufactured and traded in spice extracts, edible oils, and chemicals. Harsh Mariwala graduated from the Sydenham College of Commerce and Economics. While keen on obtaining an MBA, he did not secure admission into any Indian business schools and his father was not keen on sending him overseas; he therefore joined the family business in 1971.

While working in the family business, Harsh Mariwala noticed that they were selling unbranded edible oil in large barrels to traders who, in turn, sold it to the final consumers in small containers. He soon realized that the company was not serving consumers directly, thus losing out on high-margin sales and consumer relationships. Harsh began innovating and soon introduced Parachute brand coconut and refined edible oils in small tins, sold through a national distribution network. In 1980, Parachute tins gave way to distinctive blue plastic packs, heralding a change across the industry.

In 1990, Harsh succeeded in convincing his family to let him set up Marico as a separate entity focused on fast moving consumer goods (FMCG). Marico introduced Hair & Care, a non-sticky hair oil in 1991. In the same year, Marico took Sweekar sunflower oil across the national market. The company introduced Revive cold-water starch in 1994.

It also set up its first overseas office in Dubai and then listed on the Indian stock market in 1996. In 1999, Marico went on to establish its first overseas factory in Bangladesh. Harsh Mariwala saw an opportunity in skin-care and diversified into this area by setting up Kaya skin clinics. From the year 2000 onwards, Marico expanded through acquisitions in India and Africa as well as new product introductions in South-East Asia. Marico also entered the food domain by introducing masala oats under the Saffola brand. More recently, Marico has also diversified into self-care, wellness, and snacking by acquiring direct-to-consumer companies such as Beardo, Just Herbs, True Elements, etc.

Harsh Mariwala has set up non-profit organizations such as Mariwala Innovation Foundation to promote innovation and ASCENT Foundation to facilitate the growth of entrepreneurship. He has founded the Mariwala Health Initiative (MHI), with the philanthropic aim of giving back to society.

Forbes has estimated Harsh Mariwala's net worth to be US\$ 3.1 billion.

KEY STRATEGIES AND SUCCESS FACTORS

Strong Organizational Culture: Harsh Mariwala often quotes Peter Drucker's words, "Culture Eats Strategy for Breakfast." He has created a transparent, open culture at Marico with a sharp focus on integrity and values. The strong organizational culture at Marico allows it to compete successfully with MNCs operating in the FMCG space.

Professionalising Management: He believes that entrepreneurs should learn how to delegate by recruiting professionals who are more informed and qualified. In 2014, he stepped down from the role of Managing Director at Marico to make way for Saugata Gupta, an experienced professional.

Innovation: Harsh Mariwala is a firm believer in innovation. At Marico, he encouraged new ideas, experimentation, calculated risk-taking, and the questioning of conventional wisdom. He created an environment in which mistakes were acceptable as long and people learned from them. In his words, "Experimenting businesses never lose, only learn".

AWARDS AND RECOGNITION

- Harsh Mariwala received the Ernst & Young (EY) Entrepreneur of the Year Award in 2020
- Awarded the All-India Management Association (AIMA) Lifetime Achievement Award in 2021
- Received the Lifetime Achievement Award at the Indian Marketing Awards in 2016

An interview with

HARSH MARIWALA

Q: You have been one of the most important champions in promoting a culture of entrepreneurship in India. Your initiative Ascent Foundation is doing a commendable job in mentoring young people to become successful entrepreneurs. Based on your experience, what are the most important characteristics that an entrepreneur must possess?

A: Well, I think the first thing is a certain inclination to understand how business operates, which starts with what are the unsatisfied needs of a consumer and what can you fulfill? So, it starts with the consumer needs and how are you able to fulfill that need. Are you able to add value to that? I think the ability to identify opportunities is very important for any entrepreneur. You should be able to identify opportunities which will help you to win in the marketplace. So that's one. Number two, I think many times you may identify something, but every person has blind spots. It requires learning because the whole world is changing fast. So, openness to learn, being curious, openness to bounce off ideas is very, very important. Then the third is dealing with people in terms of your own employees, in terms of working with whoever is associated with the business. I think you should have the knack of dealing with people. And then finally you need to have that passion and resilience because every person goes through setbacks. So how do you handle setbacks? You need the determination, that drive which has

to come from within. Finally, some sort of innovative mindset because a me-too business will not succeed, you need to do something which is innovative. I would say these are the three or four things which are very crucial for any entrepreneur to succeed.

Q: In your book 'Harsh Realities' and various interviews, you have emphasized the idea of building a business for 'perpetuity'. In today's world where start-ups have such a short shelf-life, how have you created a culture in Marico that promotes 'perpetuity' and long-term thinking?

A: I think there are two things. One is every business need not think from a perpetuity point of view because many businesses can get disrupted. Depending on the kind of business you are in, the disruption could be high or low. And if the promoter is not present, something happens to him, he needs to ensure the continuity of the business. In such cases, what may happen is that the disruptor is the person who is stepping into the promoter's shoes and is not capable. Then the business can get destroyed.

So, I think this perpetuity part could or should be relevant for businesses which are relatively stable and for me the FMCG business in which Marico operates, is what is known as a defensive business. Now we are also getting disrupted but the whole world is getting disrupted with new technologies coming in, new developments coming in, and the whole world going digital. But having said that, perpetuity is the objective to continue the business from a long-term point of view.

Perpetuity means if you're not there tomorrow, the business should continue. Another is to say, okay, with me being there, how do I overcome the threats which may impact my business because of the environment?

So I think if you decide to continue the business, and I'm talking from a real long-term point of view, then you need to create certain mechanisms which will drive perpetuity.

First, you need to have a very engaged Board of Directors, a Board which looks at the leadership of the company and how capable they are. The Board looks at the culture and values of the company. The Board looks at the strategy of the company. The Board can therefore play an important role in driving perpetuity of the organization.

Now, if the perpetuity of the business is being affected by discontinuity, then you need to have a very good team that looks outside in terms of what is happening in the world which may impact you. You can have either a threat coming for your business or an opportunity. So can you look at these discontinuities from an opportunistic angle rather than threat perception?

Q. Your family was traditionally involved in the trading of spices and in the manufacture and sale of edible oils through B2B channels. You joined the business in 1971 and transformed it into a FMCG company that was primarily B2C focused. As a young man, what excited you about the B2C space that led you to drive this change?
A: I think every person is born with some strengths and all of us have some weaknesses. And this business suited me at a personal level. At that time India had the License Raj, and a lot of my friends succeeded in business by going to Delhi and getting licenses. I was not cut out for that. I was not cut out for selling in the B2B business. I am not a technical person or somebody who understands technology which this business didn't require very much of.

So in a way the FMCG business was a very good fit for what I like doing, and I was curious. I was able to identify innovations, opportunities in the consumer space. It's something which very well fitted my strengths and I didn't have to do something which I didn't like doing. But in spite of that, you go through setbacks and that's where the grit comes in. The grit is a combination of passion, combined with determination.

Q: Marico's coconut oil battle against Hindustan Unilever Ltd (HUL) in the 1990s is legendary. Your Parachute brand emerged victorious against HUL's Nihar in the marketplace thanks to your agility and tenacity. What were some of the key lessons that you learned during that battle against a strong MNC?
A: I think, first of all, you can't be dogmatic, you have to see and evaluate. To what extent can you take on a new competitor? In my case I evaluated internally. There's actually a whole chapter on that in my book 'Harsh Realities' about the threat to Marico, or threat to Parachute oil, from HUL. I went and met the owner of Nirma Detergents. We went through a lot of internal inquiry and putting ourselves into how we can take them on and try to improve wherever we could in the area of distribution, in the area of product, in the area of motivation, in the area of advertising and communication. We felt that we were able to take them on because for us this battle was everything. For HUL, Nihar was one amongst many brands which would get handled by somebody lower down the level. In our case, it would be the top management. So the fact that top management were

involved directly also played an important role in deciding to take them on. The lesson was that we should not get scared of big companies, but you need to evaluate and then decide. Small companies also have some benefits in terms of agility, in terms of quickness of decision making, in terms of their own strengths. You need to just evaluate small versus large company kind of benefits and then leverage those benefits.

Q. You have been a vocal champion of professionalisation and Marico is a professionally run company with an extremely strong talent pool. Why do you think Indian family-owned companies are often reluctant to separate ownership from management? How can this trend be changed over time to maximise stakeholder value?

A: I think this reluctance has a lot to do with Indian society which is very hierarchical. Promoters expect that their own children will inherit their business and it's so deeply ingrained. The children also think that they have a right to occupy, and society also expects that you have to put your children in your place.

But I decided that the organization's interests come first, which is good for the organization. I think my son was not ready at that time so I said that, and there was somebody else who was aspiring for this post and if we had not promoted him, he would have left. So it was in the organization's interest to give him that role and if it means that I have to step down, I should step down.

Q: Throughout your career at Marico, you have vigorously driven innovation. In fact, the Marico Innovation Foundation is a leader in recognizing game changing innovations with its 'Innovation for India Awards'. You have also been a vocal champion for the adoption of digital technology by start-ups in India. What is Marico's technology strategy in today's new digital age?

A: Technology is going to be the biggest disruptor in the next few years. You need to study how it will impact your business and what are the opportunities arising out of these technological disruptions. Many times, you may not have your own internal capability in understanding technology, so you need to get an outsider. There are many individuals or companies who can help you in terms of identifying what are the technological disruptions which may impact you, and then look at creating certain experiments in that technology. Have maybe a new team, a younger team which understands technology and let them concentrate only on technology-led disruptions. You need to remove the escape button that comes with this young team doing things other than technology.

This young, tech-savvy team must focus on the future; their work should be reviewed by the top management team to understand what's happening.

Q: You are an avid reader. Which books have influenced your journey as an entrepreneur that you would recommend to students?

A: There's not one book but many books written by Ram Charan. In earlier stages, I read a lot of books by Peter Drucker and then C.K. Prahalad. Some other books that have appealed to me are 'Grit' by Angela Duckworth, a concept which I spoke about earlier. Ram Charan's book on execution, innovation, improving Board effectiveness and Peter Drucker's books are classics in terms of management literature. I have been reading books from the time I started because I'm not an MBA so I have to learn. We recruit so many MBAs, we have some 200 MBAs so I have to be updated on management. So at a very young age, I started reading books.∎

KIRAN MAZUMDAR-SHAW

Who is **Kiran Mazumdar-Shaw?**

Kiran Mazumdar-Shaw was born on 23rd March, 1953 in Bengaluru, India. She obtained a bachelor's degree in zoology from Bangalore University and wanted to study medicine. Unfortunately, she could not get a scholarship to pursue her medical degree and she followed in her brewmaster father's footsteps and obtained a graduate degree in brewing from the University of Ballarat, Melbourne in 1975.

She was the only woman in her brewing class. Back then, brewing was a male-dominated profession in India, and this became an obstacle for Kiran; she failed to find a job as a master brewer. She worked as a consultant for a couple of years and then received a job offer to move to Scotland. Before she could leave, she met Leslie Auchincloss, the owner of Biocon Biochemicals, Ireland. He was impressed with Kiran and offered her a partnership in a new venture, Biocon India, that would make enzymes used to produce alcoholic beverages, paper, and other products. Thus, in 1978, Kiran started Biocon India in the garage of her home in Bengaluru with a seed capital of INR 10,000. Besides the challenge of poor infrastructure, she faced many daunting issues owing to the fact that she was a young woman. Employees refused to join Biocon, bankers, investors and vendors shied away. Nevertheless, Kiran persevered and within a year Biocon was making enzymes and exporting them to the US. In 1989, Auchincloss sold his Biocon India stake to Unilever. Imperial Chemical Industries (ICI) bought Unilever's specialty chemicals business along with the Biocon India stake in 1997. However, Kiran's then fiancée and future husband John Shaw personally raised US$ 2 million to buy out ICI's stake in Biocon India.

Biocon India received the US FDA approval for a cholesterol lowering molecule in 2001 and the company expanded exponentially with profits skyrocketing. It listed on the stock market in 2004 with the IPO oversubscribed 33 times. It closed the first day of trading with a market capitalization of US$ 1.11 billion.

Today, Biocon India is a fully integrated global biopharmaceutical company helping patients in 120+ countries by finding new and affordable ways to treat diabetes, cancer, and autoimmune diseases.

According to Forbes, Kiran Mazumdar-Shaw's net worth is $2.8 billion.

KEY STRATEGIES AND
SUCCESS FACTORS

Affordable Innovation: Biocon India's expansion has been driven by its philosophy of affordable innovation. Kiran Mazumdar-Shaw has always sought to provide affordable drugs in countries that are not rich and hence she has focused on low-cost alternatives and cost-effective techniques.

Compassionate Capitalism: Kiran believes that sustainable progress can be achieved through sound business models. She once said, "Innovation and commerce are as powerful tools for creating social progress as they are for driving technological advancement. When they are put to use for social progress, the implementation is a lot cheaper, a lot more people benefit, and the effect is more lasting." Kiran signed The Giving Pledge in 2015, promising that at least half of her wealth will be dedicated to philanthropy.

Global Footprint: Biocon products are available in over 120 countries. With a strong overseas footprint, the company has been successful in diversifying its revenue sources, thus reducing its reliance on the Indian market.

AWARDS AND RECOGNITION

- Kiran Mazumdar-Shaw received India's third highest civilian honour, the Padma Bhushan in 2005
- Awarded India's fourth highest civilian honour, Padma Shri in 1989
- Received Australia's highest civilian honour, the Order of Australia in 2020
- She was named Ernst & Young (EY) World Entrepreneur of The Year in 2020
- Awarded the Othmer Gold Medal for outstanding contributions to the progress of science and chemistry in 2014
- Received the Businesswoman of The Year Award from The Economic Times in 2004

SUNIL MITTAL

Who is **Sunil Mittal?**

Sunil Mittal was born on 23rd October, 1957 in Ludhiana, Punjab. His father Sat Paul Mittal was a politician from the state of Punjab and was a Rajya Sabha Member for three terms. Sunil obtained his Bachelor of Arts degree from Punjab University in 1976. Later in his life, he completed the Owner/President Management (OPM) program from Harvard Business School in 1999.

From a young age, Sunil was inclined towards entrepreneurship. At the age of 18, he borrowed INR 20,000 from his father and started a business manufacturing bicycle crankshafts. In 1980, he and his brothers Rakesh and Rajan Mittal, established Bharti Overseas Trading. Given that import was tightly controlled during the License Raj, Sunil purchased import licenses from exporters in Punjab who obtained them in lieu of their exports. He used these licenses to import Suzuki's portable electric gensets from Japan. Unfortunately for him, in 1983, the import of gensets was banned by the Government and his business was seriously impacted. Not one to give up easily, he began importing push-button telephones from Taiwan to replace traditional rotary telephones and marketed them under the Beetel brand. Sunil saw tremendous scope in the telecom business, and in 1984 he set up Bharti Telecom Ltd to assemble push-button phones in India in collaboration with Siemens of Germany. By the early 1990s, he was manufacturing fax machines, push-button phones, and other telecom gear for the Indian market.

Telecom was booming globally and the Indian Government invited bids for mobile phone network licenses. In 1992, Sunil won one of the four mobile telephony licenses auctioned by the Government. One of the conditions was that the winner should be experienced in mobile telephony. Sunil entered into an alliance with the French telecom group Vivendi; he set up Bharti Cellular Ltd to launch mobile telephony services in Delhi & Himachal Pradesh under the brand name Airtel. He has been very successful in establishing strategic partnerships with leading global players such as British Telecom, Singapore Telecom, IBM Global Services, etc. In June 2010, Sunil acquired the African operations of Kuwait's Zain Telecom for US$ 10.7 billion. While his African business struggled initially, today Airtel Africa is profitable and is a leading provider of telecom services in 14 African countries. Airtel Africa is listed on the LSE.

Airtel is the second largest telco in India based on the number of its subscribers and market share. Sunil Mittal's Bharti Enterprises is also the largest shareholder in Eutelsat Group, a global leader in satellite communications and he serves as Co-Chair of the company.

Forbes estimates Sunil Bharti Mittal and his family's net worth to be US$ 16.8 billion.

KEY STRATEGIES AND SUCCESS FACTORS

Strategic Partnerships: Strategic partnerships have been at the forefront of Sunil Mittal's success. His ability to forge alliances with companies such as Vivendi, British Telecom, Singapore Telecom, IBM Global Services etc, have allowed Airtel to expand its reach, develop expertise, and innovate. Google invested US$1 billion in Airtel in January 2022.

Overseas Expansion: One of Sunil Mittal's most audacious bets was his overseas expansion into Africa. He acquired Zain Telecom's Africa business for US$ 10.7 billion. The business struggled for some time but today Airtel Africa is the continent's second largest telecom provider.

Modular Approach: Sunil Mittal adopted a unique modular approach while entering the capital-intensive telecom sector. Many small businesses shied away from investing in telecom because it required large financial investments. His modular approach entailed establishing the network in parts. In his words, "You can start with a 10,000-line exchange and a few base stations, and then go from there, depending on your performance."

AWARDS AND RECOGNITION

- Sunil Bharti Mittal was awarded India's third highest civilian award, the Padma Bhushan in 2007
- Awarded an honorary knighthood (KBE) by King Charles III of the United Kingdom in 2024
- Named Business Leader of the Year at The Economic Times Awards for Corporate Excellence in 2022
- Received the INSEAD Business Leader Award in 2011
- Conferred Ernst & Young (EY) Entrepreneur of the Year Award in 2004
- Conferred Business Leader of the Year Award by Economic Times in 2005
- Named CEO of the Year by Business Standard for 2005-06
- Received Asia Businessman of the Year Award from Fortune in 2006
- Received US-India Business Council (USIBC) Global Vision Award in 2008

NR NARAYANA **MURTHY**

Who is **NR Narayana Murthy?**

NR Narayana Murthy was born on 21st August, 1946 in a middle-class family in Sidlaghatta, Karnataka. He attended a government school and obtained his Bachelor's degree in electrical engineering from the University of Mysore and Master's degree from IIT Kanpur in 1969.

After completing his education, Narayana Murthy began his career at IIM Ahmedabad as Chief Systems Programmer. He then joined SESA, Paris from 1972-1974 helping develop the software to handle air cargo at Charles de Gaulle Airport. After returning to India, he started a software company named Softronics which failed in a short time. He then joined Patni Computer Systems and worked there for 5 years.

In 1981, Narayana Murthy co-founded Infosys with 6 other professionals. His initial capital investment in Infosys was INR 10,000 which was provided by his wife Sudha Murty. Infosys aimed at providing custom software development for companies worldwide.

India had not yet liberalized and Infosys grew slowly till 1991. Once the economy opened up, Narayana Murthy moved rapidly to expand the company's international client base and provide them with consulting, systems integration, software development, and product engineering services. In fact, he conceptualized, articulated, and implemented the Global Delivery Model (GDM) which went on to become the foundation of the Indian software sector.

As a result, in the 1990s Infosys acquired marquee global clients like Citigroup, Cisco Systems, Dell, Gap, and Aetna.

Narayana Murthy took Infosys public in 1993; in 2004 Infosys listed on NASDAQ becoming the first Indian company to list on an American stock exchange.

He served as CEO of Infosys from 1981 – 2002 and later became Chairman of the company between 2002 - 2011. He returned as Executive Chairman between 2013 and 2014 to help the company during a difficult time.

Forbes estimates Narayana Murthy's net worth to be US\$ 4.9 billion.

AWARDS AND RECOGNITION

- NR Narayana Murthy received India's second highest civilian award, the Padma Vibhushan in 2008
- Awarded the CBE by the United Kingdom in 2007
- Awarded the Legion of Honour by France in 2008
- Received the Ernst & Young (EY) World Entrepreneur Award in 2003
- Received India's third highest civilian award, the Padma Shri in 2000

KEY STRATEGIES AND **SUCCESS FACTORS**

Innovation: Narayana Murthy is a big proponent of innovation. In fact, he conceptualized the Global Delivery Model (GDM) which allowed Infosys to serve customers worldwide. The GDM laid the foundation of India's software industry. In his words, "The most important thing you people have to do is to create an idea whose differentiated business value proposition is better than any of your competitors. You must think of differentiation at all times. And that differentiation is going to come because of innovation."

Being a Values-Based Organization: According to Narayana Murthy, Infosys always focused on being a values-based organization. Infosys was not willing to compromise on its integrity by paying bribes. While this approach posed short term challenges and caused delays in the early days, in the long run it gave Infosys a big advantage. Knowing that Infosys would not cut corners, global clients were willing to trust the company with large projects resulting in higher revenue growth. Investors were willing to invest in Infosys because of its strong corporate governance and employees were happy working for a company where they could follow the right path.

Sustainable Financial Model: Narayana Murthy believes that austerity and financial discipline have helped Infosys succeed. According to him, all companies should be based on a sustainable financial model. Entrepreneurs must have a business plan of 5 years, extendable up to 7-10 years, to become profitable in their ventures. For the past several years, he has called out the fact that VCs would not be able to pump money into loss-making businesses forever.

SHIV NADAR

Who is **Shiv Nadar?**

Shiv Nadar was born on 14th July, 1945, in a coastal village in southern Tamil Nadu. Despite having limited resources and facing financial difficulties, he pursued his pre-university degree from The American College, Madurai, and an electrical and electronics engineering degree on a scholarship from the PSG College of Technology, Coimbatore. Nadar's education was primarily in the Tamil language, and he didn't start speaking much English until age 22.

Nadar began his career at the Walchand Group's Cooper Engineering, Pune in 1967 and in the same year secured a job in Delhi Cloth Mills (DCM). After working at DCM's digital division for a few years, he along with a few colleagues, realized that they wanted to be entrepreneurs and follow their passion. They left DCM in 1976 to found Microcomp with a small investment to sell teledigital calculators. Shiv Nadar was the largest shareholder in Microcomp. Their timing was impeccable as the Government and IBM were engaged in a tussle and IBM exited India in 1978.

Impressed with the vision of Shiv Nadar and his co-founders, the Uttar Pradesh Government gave him INR 2 million for a 26% stake, which they used along with the profit from Microcomp to found Hindustan Computers Limited (HCL). This was the one of the first Public-Private Partnerships (PPP) in India. Early in its existence, HCL introduced India's first personal computer called the HCL 8C; in 1979, he took the business overseas with a foray into Singapore. The company moved into IT software services in 1991 and is one of India's largest software service providers today. When Shiv Nadar retired as the Chairman of HCL Technologies in July 2020, the company had a global revenue of US$ 11.9 billion.

Shiv Nadar is not just admired for his visionary entrepreneurship; he is equally celebrated for his initiatives in education and philanthropy to which he has committed over US$ 1 billion.

Today, he serves as Chairman Emeritus of HCL Technologies and Shiv Nadar Foundation.

Forbes estimates Shiv Nadar's net worth to be US$ 36.1 billion.

AWARDS AND RECOGNITION

- Shiv Nadar was awarded India's third highest civilian award, the Padma Bhushan in 2008
- Received The Economic Times Lifetime Achievement Award for Corporate Excellence in 2022
- Received the USISPF Lifetime Achievement Award from US-India Strategic Partnership Forum in 2022
- Featured among the Forbes 48 Heroes of Philanthropy in Asia-Pacific in 2011

KEY STRATEGIES AND
SUCCESS FACTORS

Hire the Best Talent: Shiv Nadar always made it a point to hire the best talent. Even in its early days, HCL used to hire from the IITs and IIMs offering higher salaries than even Citibank. Shiv Nadar liked to bring on team members who were aggressive, passionate, intelligent and then give them the environment to succeed. This helped HCL grow rapidly. This was also the reason that HCL became a breeding ground for CEOs of India's IT industry and for successful entrepreneurs.

Innovation: Shiv Nadar's focus on innovation cemented HCL's technological prowess and the company continues to walk on this path with several global R&D partnerships and innovation labs. He also co-founded NIIT in 1981 to help the nascent IT industry overcome its human resource challenges by creating a new generation of computer-savvy individuals. This was truly far sighted.

Focus on the Greater Good: He founded the Shiv Nadar Foundation in 1994 which has played a big role in developing India's education infrastructure. In 2022, Shiv Nadar was declared India's most generous man; during the year he donated an average of INR 30 million (US$ 360,000) per day, mostly towards educational causes.

FALGUNI **NAYAR**

Who is **Falguni Nayar?**

Falguni Nayar was born on 19th February, 1963 in Mumbai in a Gujarati family. Her father was a businessman who ran a small bearings company and her mother assisted in the business. She completed her B.Com from Mumbai's Sydenham College, and then obtained her post graduate degree in management from IIM Ahmedabad in 1985. She went on to join AF Ferguson & Co as a management consultant and spent over 8 years at the firm. She then moved to the Kotak Mahindra Group, going on to open offices in London and New York for its institutional equities business, before returning to India in 2001 to head Kotak's overall institutional equities business. She also took on additional responsibility becoming Managing Director of the Kotak's investment banking business, leading the firm to become India's leading IPO banker and playing a prominent role in some of India's largest M&A transactions. She was part of Kotak's operating management committee, a small group of top management.

While she was extremely successful at Kotak, Falguni was clear that she wanted to become an entrepreneur before she turned 50. She observed the massive untapped potential of the beauty and personal care products market in India. Driven by higher internet penetration, India's e-commerce market had also begun to grow rapidly. Hence, Falguni quit Kotak and founded Nykaa in 2012 with her own savings. The name was inspired by the Sanskrit word 'Nayaka' which means 'one in the spotlight.'

Falguni's vision was to build Nykaa as a multi-brand, omnichannel beauty-focused retail business. She wanted to empower customers across India by providing them access to previously unavailable, high-quality beauty and personal care products. Nykaa gave customers the opportunity to buy over 35,000 products from 850 brands on its platform, which revolutionised the Indian beauty products industry. Keeping in mind her omnichannel vision, Falguni also drove Nykaa's physical presence, launching its first brick and mortar store in 2015. The brand has over 140 stores in India today and aims to further expand its offline presence. It has also diversified into new categories such as Fast Fashion.

Nykaa's IPO in 2021 was oversubscribed 82.5 times, and the firm was valued at nearly US$ 13 billion on the day of its listing.

Forbes estimates Falguni Nayar's net worth to be US$ 2.9 billion.

AWARDS AND RECOGNITION

- Falguni Nayar received the Ernst & Young (EY) Entrepreneur of the Year Award in 2021
- Received the CEO of the Year Award at The Economic Times Start-up Awards in 2022
- Honored with the Dataquest Pathbreaker of the Year Award in 2021
- Received the DNA Women Achievers Award in 2023

KEY STRATEGIES AND
SUCCESS FACTORS

Spotting the Opportunity Early: Falguni Nayar was quick to observe the massive untapped potential of the beauty products market in India. However, her observation was not arbitrary; it took into account the growth in e-commerce brands such as Flipkart due to increasing internet penetration. She also perfectly understood the pulse of Indian women - their higher aspirations and desire to step into the spotlight in their own lives.

Omnichannel Approach: Though she launched Nykaa as an online platform, Falguni quickly sensed that Indian women (particularly in Tier 2 and 3 cities) were more comfortable in 'seeing and buying' beauty and personal care products. Since customers were unable to try products on Nykaa's online platform, she introduced brick and mortar stores in 2015. Nykaa currently operates over 140 stores in India and plans to expand to over 300 stores across 100 cities.

Effective Digital Marketing and Tech Deployment: One of the biggest factors behind Nykaa's success is its marketing strategy. Nykaa's target audience skews young, and it has successfully created a large digital presence through influencer marketing, celebrity make-up and beauty blogs, and SEO. It has also leveraged technology effectively to create an immersive and personalized online buying experience for consumers. Nykaa has deployed analytics to glean customer insights that help drive its product curation, assortment and pricing decisions. This translates into brand loyalty and repeat business for Nykaa from its existing customers.

BALVANT **PAREKH**

Who is **Balvant Parekh?**

Balvant Parekh was born in 1925 in Mahuva, Gujarat. His family was very keen that he pursue law. He moved to Mumbai to study at the Government Law College, obtained his law degree and cleared the bar council exams.

He chose not to practice law. He worked in a printing and dyeing press and then as a peon in a wood trader's office. He soon decided to set up his own business and with an investor he began importing cycles, paper, nuts and other commodities.

Balvant Parekh got a break when he became a 50% partner with Fedco, a firm that represented Hoechst in India. After a while, due to circumstances beyond his control, Hoechst wanted to operate independently in India.

In 1954, along with his brother Sushil, Balvant set up Parekh Dye-Chem in Mumbai that traded and manufactured dyes, industrial chemicals, and pigment emulsions. He saw that there was a gap in the Indian adhesive market because existing glues were weak and also were made from animal parts. India needed a 'vegetarian glue' and Balvant soon started manufacturing a strong glue made from synthetic resin and named it 'Fevicol'. He targeted Fevicol at carpenters who were the biggest buyers and decision makers when it came to adhesive purchases. In 1959, the company was renamed as Pidilite Industries.

Today Pidilite produces adhesives, sealants, waterproofing solutions, construction chemicals, industrial resins, polymers, arts & craft products, etc.

The market capitalization of Pidilite today stands at US$ 16.5 billion.

AWARDS AND RECOGNITION

- Balvant Parekh was the first Asian to receive the prestigious J Talbot Winchell Award from the Institute of General Semantics in 2011

KEY STRATEGIES AND
SUCCESS FACTORS

Consumer Focus: Pidilite began with industrial products - dyes, industrial chemicals and pigments. Due to Balvant Parekh's brilliant insight about the gap in the adhesive market, it began manufacturing Fevicol, first targeted at carpenters. Over the years, Pidilite has evolved into one of India's most consumer-focused companies and dominates the country's adhesives market.

Strong Distribution Network and Global Presence: Under Balvant Parekh's leadership, Pidilite established an extremely wide distribution network. Today, the company has 6,000 distributors and 600,000 dealers / retailers across India. Pidilite exports products to over 80 countries. It has 20 overseas subsidiaries and manufacturing facilities in USA, Thailand, Dubai, Brazil, Egypt, Bangladesh, Sri Lanka, and Kenya.

Branding and Advertising: The Fevicol brand is associated with quirky, humorous and contemporary advertising. Pidilite and the creative agency Ogilvy have worked together for several decades to create the Fevicol brand that is synonymous with adhesives and glue in India. Whether advertised on television, print or the internet, Pidilite's various brands stand out amidst the clutter.

DEEPAK **PAREKH**

Who is **Deepak Parekh?**

Deepak Parekh was born on 18th October, 1944 in Mumbai in a family of bankers. He obtained his B.Com degree from Sydenham College and went to England in 1965 to qualify as a Chartered Accountant. He also obtained the CAIIB degree from the Indian Institute of Banking & Finance (IIBF). He then worked with Ernst & Young, Grindlays, and Chase Manhattan Bank.

His journey with Housing Development Finance Corporation Ltd (HDFC) commenced in 1978 after he was convinced by HT Parekh (his uncle and HDFC founder) to join the company.

Initially, housing finance was a foreign concept in India, but HDFC survived by raising long-term resources from the World Bank, IFC, and USAID. Deepak Parekh quickly rose through the ranks at HDFC and became Managing Director in 1985. He led HDFC safely through the oil crisis caused by the first Gulf War and became Chairman of HDFC in 1993.

In 1993, HDFC successfully applied for a banking license from RBI and incorporated HDFC Bank which is India's most valuable lender today. HDFC set up several joint ventures including HDFC Life (2000) and HDFC Ergo (2002). In April 2022, Deepak Parekh announced that HDFC would merge with HDFC Bank creating a financial services giant valued at US$ 160 billion.

Deepak Parekh has helped the Government resolve various crises such as the Satyam scam. He is an active member of various high-powered Economic Groups, Government-appointed Advisory Committees and Task Forces. He continues to serve as a director on several company boards.

AWARDS AND RECOGNITION

- Deepak Parekh received India's third highest civilian award, the Padma Bhushan in 2006
- Received the 'Bundesverdienstkreuz' (Cross of the Order of Merit) from the German Government in 2014
- Received the Lifetime Achievement Award from The Economic Times in 2012
- Was the first international recipient of The Institute of Chartered Accountants of England and Wales' (ICAEW) Outstanding Achievement Award in 2010
- Received the Businessman of the Year award from Business India in 1996

KEY STRATEGIES AND SUCCESS FACTORS

Building the Right Human Capital: Deepak Parekh has an uncanny knack for selecting the right kind of executives to get the job done. This has added significant value to each subsidiary of the HDFC Group. For instance, getting Aditya Puri to lead HDFC Bank in 1994 and Amitabh Chaudhry to lead HDFC Standard Life in 2010 were astute moves because both entities have become leaders in their own sectors.

Trust and Integrity: Deepak Parekh is known for his integrity and this permeates through HDFC. He says, "Guard against greed, excess leverage and short-cuts. Honesty, integrity and humility are time-tested traits and there is no softer pillow to lay your head upon at night than a clear conscience."

Diversification: To take advantage of deregulation in the financial sector, Deepak Parekh effectively diversified HDFC into growth sectors such as banking, life insurance and general insurance. HDFC Bank is India's most valuable lender; HDFC Standard Life has a market share of 18.4% in life insurance and HDFC Ergo's market share is 6.1% in the general insurance sector.

AJAY **PIRAMAL**

Who is **Ajay Piramal?**

Ajay Piramal was born on 20th December, 1955 in Bagar, Rajasthan. His family was involved in the textile business; his father continued the textile business established by Ajay's grandfather, Seth Piramal Chaturbhuj Makharia. After completing his MBA from Jamnalal Bajaj Institute of Management Studies, Mumbai, at the age of 22, Ajay joined his his father's textile business. The business was run by Ajay's father and his two brothers Dilip and Ashok, both of whom were elder to him. Following their father's death in 1979, Dilip Piramal separated from the business to independently run VIP Industries and Blow Plast while Ajay and Ashok continued to run the textile business. Unfortunately, Ashok passed away in 1984 and Ajay was pushed into the leadership position in Morarjee Mills (his grandfather's cotton mill) amidst the largest textile industry strike in India. In essence, what he inherited seemed to be a bleak future but as they say, fortune favours the brave, and he courageously steered the group to new heights.

Over the years, Ajay Piramal has acquired the reputation of being India's 'takeover man'. He is known for his acumen in buying businesses at the right price, building and then selling them at a handsome profit. For example, in the 1980s he bought a small pharmaceuticals company which he grew for three decades before selling it to the MNC Abbott Laboratories for US$ 3.72 billion in 2010.

In 2021, the Group's finance company Piramal Capital & Housing Finance Ltd acquired the distressed lender DHFL for US$ 4.6 billion in cash and bonds. Today, the Piramal Group has a strong presence in pharmaceuticals, realty and finance. The Piramal Foundation drives the Group's philanthropic initiatives.

Forbes estimates Ajay Piramal's net worth to be US$ 4.4 billion.

AWARDS AND RECOGNITION

- Ajay Piramal was honored with the CBE by Queen Elizabeth II for his services to the UK-India trade relationship in 2022
- Received the 'Deal Maker Hall Of Fame' Award at the Mint India Investment Summit in March 2022
- The Ajay Piramal Family won the 'Distinguished Family of the Year' by Forbes Philanthropy in 2014 for dedicating their wealth towards social good
- Was declared as the Indian Innovator of the Year by CNBC-TV18 in 2008
- Was named Global Leader of Tomorrow by the World Economic Forum in 2004

KEY STRATEGIES AND
SUCCESS FACTORS

Mergers and Acquisitions: Ajay Piramal is known for his knack of finding and acquiring companies that are hidden gems. Therefore, acquisitions over the years have driven the diversification of the Piramal Group and its rapid growth. The latest example is his US$ 4.6 billion acquisition of the distressed lender DHFL. He also has the uncanny ability to divest businesses at great valuations after building them.

Long-term Trust: Ajay Piramal has on many occasions cited the importance of trust, especially in mergers, acquisitions and collaborations. His focus on trust and long term relationships make him the partner of choice for many global MNCs.

Philanthropy: A deeply spiritual person, Ajay Piramal is focused on 'Doing Well and Doing Good', a philosophy that has created long-term value for the Piramal Group's stakeholders and the community as a whole.

CYRUS **POONAWALLA**

Who is **Dr. Cyrus Poonawalla?**

Cyrus Poonawalla was born on 11th May, 1941 in Pune, India. His father was a horse breeder, and the family owned a stud farm in Pune. Poonawalla studied at Bishops School in Pune and went on to graduate from Brihan Maharashtra College of Commerce (BMCC) in 1966. In 1988, he was awarded a Ph.D. by the Pune University; his thesis was titled 'Improved Technology in the manufacture of specific Anti-toxins and its socio-economic impact on Society'.

As a young man, Poonawalla realized that horse racing had, "no future in the socialist India of the time" and began exploring other business opportunities. He was passionate about automobiles and along with a school friend, he built a US$ 120 prototype car that was based on the Jaguar Model D. However, due to lack of finance for commercial production, he dropped the idea. Poonawalla then decided that he would work on developing products that would cater to India's masses, rather than the elite.

India imported expensive vaccines for meeting the country's healthcare requirements. The Government's Haffkine Institute in Mumbai manufactured some vaccines from serum extracted from retired horses that Poonawalla's stud farm donated to it. Based on a conversation with a vet at the family's stud farm, Poonawalla recognised that he could meet the demand for vaccines in India by extracting the serum from horses himself. He established the Serum Institute of India (SII) in 1966 with an investment of only US$ 12,000.

Within 2 years of being founded, SII launched its first therapeutic anti-tetanus serum, and began producing anti-tetanus vaccines. SII introduced the DTP vaccine in 1974, and an anti-snake-venom serum in 1981, followed by a measles vaccine in 1989. By 1990, SII was India's largest vaccine manufacturer. It was accredited by WHO to export vaccines in 1994 and began supplying high quality vaccines to various UN agencies. Today, SII is the world's largest vaccine maker (by number of doses), producing over 1.5 billion doses annually. SII's Covishield, the vaccine developed by AstraZeneca and Oxford University, was the most widely used in India during the Covid pandemic.

Dr. Cyrus Poonawalla serves as Chairman of SII, while his son Adar serves as its CEO. The Cyrus Poonawalla Group also has a majority stake in the listed financial services company Poonawalla Fincorp.

Forbes estimates Dr. Cyrus Poonawalla's net worth to be US$ 25.5 billion.

KEY STRATEGIES AND
SUCCESS FACTORS

Focus on the Greater Good: Dr. Cyrus Poonawala's goal to create affordable vaccines and serve people has driven SII's approach towards business. His commitment to "Health for All with affordable Vaccines" has resulted in several partnerships such as those with WHO and Bill & Melinda Gates Foundation that focus on providing affordable vaccines to developing countries, and those in need.

Build a Strong Team and Establish Collaborations: Poonawala himself did not come from a medical background. Hence he placed great emphasis on building a strong team that included the best doctors and scientists. He also established partnerships with several biotech companies and institutes for developing expertise. This approach has helped SII tremendously in research & development and creating a culture of innovation.

High Volume, Low Prices: Dr. Cyrus Poonawala's business model has always focused on comparative advantage. SII produces vaccines in high volumes at low prices. This gives the company a significant edge over competitors while driving sustainable, long-term revenue streams.

AWARDS AND RECOGNITION

- Dr. Cyrus Poonawalla received India's third highest civilian award, the Padma Bhushan in 2022
- Received India's fourth highest civilian award, the Padma Shri in 2005
- Awarded the Dean's Medal from the Johns Hopkins Bloomberg School of Public Health in 2022
- Received the Sabin Humanitarian Award and Sabin Global Corporate Philanthropy Award in 2005 from the Sabin Vaccine Institute, USA
- Awarded Ernst and Young (EY) Entrepreneur of the Year for India in 2014
- Received Ernst and Young (EY) Entrepreneur of the Year in Healthcare and Life Sciences in 2007
- Granted Honorary Degree of Doctor of Humane Letters by University of Massachusetts in 2018
- Conferred with the 'Degree of Doctor of Science, honoris causa' by the University of Oxford in 2019
- Conferred the Lokmanya Tilak National Award in 2021
- Awarded ICMR Lifetime Achievement Medal for contribution to healthcare in 2019

AZIM PREMJI

Who is **Azim Premji?**

Azim Premji was born on the 24th July, 1945 in Mumbai. His father was a prominent businessman whose company Western India Vegetable Products Ltd made cooking oil, hydrogenated vegetable oil, etc.

After he completed his schooling in Mumbai, Azim Premji went to Stanford University to study engineering. Unfortunately, his father passed away suddenly in 1966 just before Azim Premji completed his graduation, and he had to return to India to take over the family business. He was only 21 years old at that time. He diversified the company's product line to include bakery fats, toiletries, light bulbs, hair care products, and hydraulic cylinders. In 1978, the Government of India expelled the technology giant IBM from India. Azim Premji immediately recognized the opportunity of serving the nascent computer hardware and software market and pivoted to information technology, manufacturing mini-computers in collaboration with Sentinel Computer Corporation, US. He renamed his company as Wipro and soon diversified into software as well.

Employing qualified Indians, Wipro was successful in developing high-quality software at much lower costs when compared to the US. Wipro began developing and exporting customized software to companies in the West. Wipro listed on the New York Stock Exchange (NYSE) in the year 2000. India's economic liberalization in the early 1990s unshackled the economy, and helped Wipro cross a billion dollars in revenue in 2004. In FY23, Wipro's annual revenue was greater than US$ 11 billion and its market capitalization stands at US$ 31 billion today.

A frugal and modest man, Azim Premji is also recognized as one of India's greatest philanthropists, focusing on education. He set up the Azim Premji Foundation in 2001 and has pledged endowments of over US$ 21 billion to social causes. He was the first Indian to sign The Giving Pledge. Azim Premji officially completed his engineering degree from Stanford in 1999, over 30 years after having had to drop out.

Forbes estimates Azim Premji's net worth to be US$ 11.9 billion.

AWARDS AND RECOGNITION

- Azim Premji was awarded India's second highest civilian honour, the Padma Vibhushan in 2011
- Has been bestowed with the highest French civilian distinction Knight of the Legion of Honour in 2018
- Was bestowed with India's third highest civilian honour, the Padma Bhushan in 2005
- Was the first Indian to receive the prestigious Faraday Medal in 2005 for his contribution towards elementary education in India
- In 2019, Forbes featured Azim Premji in the list of the world's most generous philanthropists outside the US
- Received the Carnegie Medal of Philanthropy in 2017

KEY STRATEGIES AND SUCCESS FACTORS

Culture of Innovation: According to Azim Premji, "It is impossible to generate a few good ideas without a lot of bad ideas. Failure should be forgiven and forgotten quickly." Wipro designed a culture of innovation to actively seek feedback from customers, celebrate all kinds of diversity in its workforce, and also foster an environment in which workers feel safe taking risks, even when they fail.

Focus on People: Wipro's success has been built on the shoulders of its people. When Wipro diversified into IT, Azim Premji focused on recruiting the best software developers in India and providing excellent training to them. Wipro was one of India's first companies to offer ESOPs and help its team members build wealth. Azim Premji created a very empowering environment for his team. This helped Wipro differentiate itself from competition, especially in the early days of India's IT Revolution.

Integrity: Azim Premji is known for his very strong sense of integrity, which is a key value enshrined in the 'Spirit of Wipro' as follows:

"Integrity is our core and is the basis of everything. It is about following the law, but it's more. It is about delivering on our commitments. It is about honesty and fairness in action. It is about being ethical beyond any doubt, in the toughest of circumstances."

RAJAN **RAHEJA**

Who is **Rajan Raheja?**

Rajan Raheja was born in 1953 in Mumbai into a prominent business family. His father Dr. Biharilal S. Raheja ran a large real estate development company. After completing his graduation, Rajan Raheja joined the family's real estate business.

After a family split, he ventured out on his own by forming the Rajan Raheja group. He set up a real estate company named R. Raheja Properties in 1981.

In 1989, he entered into a joint venture with the Taparia family of Supreme Industries to set up Supreme Petrochem Ltd.

He entered the building materials sector by setting up a cement company named Karan Cement Ltd in 1992; this was renamed as Prism Cement in 1994. To strengthen his presence in this sector, Rajan Raheja acquired the ceramic tile manufacturer H&R Johnson (India) in 1993. He partnered with the RMC Group plc, UK in 1994 to set up RMC Readymix

India to make ready-mix concrete. In 2004, RMC Readymix India became a 100% subsidiary of the Rajan Raheja Group. Today, the Group's building materials businesses (cement, RMC, ceramic tiles) are housed in Prism Johnson Ltd.

Rajan Raheja's masterstroke was the expansion into batteries in 1993 through the acquisition of Associate Battery Makers (Eastern) later renamed Exide Industries Ltd. Exide is now India's largest selling battery company.

Besides the above, the Rajan Raheja Group has interests in software (Sonata Software), publishing (Outlook magazine), hotels, insurance, and asset management.

Forbes estimates Rajan Raheja and family's net worth to be US$ 4.3 billion.

KEY STRATEGIES AND
SUCCESS FACTORS

Diversification: Rajan Raheja's diversification strategy is evident from the range of sectors into which he has successfully diversified. He correctly identified growth industries and sectors and entered these at the right time.

Joint Ventures and Partnerships: Rajan Raheja has strategically used partnerships and joint ventures to drive the growth of his group in a variety of sectors. For example, the JV with the Taparia family in the petrochem space - Supreme Petrochem Ltd, similarly the general insurance JV with QBE, the hospitality venture promoted with the Oberoi family - EIH Associated Hotels Ltd, etc.

Mergers & Acquisitions: Rajan Raheja is extremely adept at mergers and acquisitions. Whether it is his acquisition of Exide Industries or his decision to sell the Group's stake in Exide Life to HDFC Life in 2022, he deploys M&A very strategically to further his group's interests.

SHASHI & RAVI **RUIA**

Who are **Shashi & Ravi Ruia?**

Shashi and Ravi Ruia were born in Mumbai in 1944 and 1949 respectively. They came from a business family and their father Nand Kishore Ruia was involved in the construction business before moving to Chennai to set up an exports business in the 1950s.

After their father's passing in 1969, the brothers took over the business and laid the foundation of the modern Essar Group. India's economic liberalization in the 1990s brought several opportunities. Led by them, Essar diversified into industries like oil & gas, steel, shipping, and telecom. Essar played a large role in building India's ports, refineries, steel plants, and mobile network infrastructure. The Group also expanded its interests overseas to US, Canada and Europe.

In 2008, Essar had commenced a US$ 30 billion investment program across its businesses. However, the years 2010-2015 saw Essar facing several adverse legal and government actions including the cancellation of critical natural gas supply and coal mine allocations. This resulted in the Group facing significant financial difficulties and excessive leverage.

In order to pare its mounting debt, Essar undertook a deleveraging program, monetizing assets to raise resources:

- Essar Oil was taken over by Rosneft and Trafigura for US$ 12.9 billion
- Aegis BPO was sold for US$ 300 million
- Essar Steel was taken over by ArcelorMittal in 2019 after a 2 year battle in the bankruptcy courts and became ArcelorMittal Nippon Steel
- In 2022, Essar Group agreed to sell 3 ports, 2 power plants and a power transmission line to ArcelorMittal Nippon Steel for US$ 2.4 billion

Essar has completed its deleveraging program and repaid its debt of US$ 25 billion to Indian banks. In its current avatar, Essar Global Fund Limited (EGFL), set up in 2005, owns the businesses that Shashi and Ravi Ruia co-founded. EGFL is a global investor and owns assets across core sectors of energy, metals & mining, infrastructure, technology and services.

EGFL's portfolio companies generate aggregate revenues of US $15 billion.

AWARDS AND RECOGNITION

Shashi Ruia
- Received the Businessman of the Year Award from Business India in 2010
- Awarded an honorary fellowship by Institute of Marine Engineers India
- Was the Chairman of the Indo-US Joint Business Council in 2013

Ravi Ruia
- Received the Businessman of the Year Award from Business India in 2010
- Was awarded the Outstanding Contribution to Sustainability Award at The Asian Awards in London in 2013

KEY STRATEGIES AND **SUCCESS FACTORS**

Diversification: Shashi and Ravi Ruia led Essar's diversification into different core sectors of India's economy such as energy, metals, infrastructure, etc. Diversification helped Essar to grow rapidly during the economic liberalization of the 1990s. In fact, Essar played a large role in building India's ports, refineries, steel plants, and mobile network infrastructure.

Grit and Perseverance: The Ruia brothers embody these qualities that are critical for any entrepreneur. Operating in highly capital-intensive, cyclical and regulated sectors, the Group's companies have had to face financial stress on more than one occasion. Despite their recent challenges, the Ruias are rebuilding various businesses in the Group.

Globalisation: Early on, the Ruia brothers understood the importance of taking the Essar Group to the global stage to benefit from global investments. They developed global relationships that have helped the Group tremendously. Over the years, Shashi and Ravi Ruia have entered into very large deals with global giants such as Rosneft, Trafigura, Vodafone for their companies across sectors. For example, the sale of Essar Oil to Rosneft and Trafigura for US$ 12.9 billion is considered as one of the largest Foreign Direct Investments (FDIs) in India's energy sector.

DILIP **SHANGHVI**

Who is **Dilip Shanghvi?**

Dilip Shanghvi was born on 1st October, 1955 at Amreli in Gujarat. His father was a wholesaler of pharmaceuticals, mainly generic drugs. He studied at the JJ Ajmera High School and obtained his bachelor's degree in commerce from the Bhawanipur Education Society, Kolkata. Dilip Shanghvi began helping his father in his pharmaceuticals business and realized that he should be involved in the manufacturing of drugs.

In 1982, he set up his first manufacturing unit at Vapi, Gujarat with an investment of INR 10,000. The company was named Sun Pharmaceuticals and manufactured a few psychiatric drugs. By the early 1990s, Sun had set up research facilities and was also manufacturing drugs for gastroenterology and cardiology.

Sun Pharma launched its IPO in 1994 and then proceeded to make its first overseas acquisition, US-based Caraco Pharmaceutical Laboratories; Sun also acquired stakes in Tamil Nadu Dadha Pharmaceuticals and MJ Pharmaceuticals in India. Dilip Shanghvi continued to acquire companies and brands between 1999 and 2012. After a bruising three year battle, he successfully acquired Taro Pharmaceutical Industries, doubling Sun's US revenues to US$ 1 billion.

In 2015, Dilip Shanghvi acquired rival Ranbaxy Laboratories for US$ 3.2 billion from Daiichi Sankyo Co, Japan. With this acquisition, Sun became the world's fourth largest generic drug producer and the largest pharma company in India.

Forbes estimates Dilip Shanghvi's net worth to be US$ 24.9 billion.

AWARDS AND RECOGNITION

- Dilip Shanghvi received India's fourth highest civilian award, the Padma Shri in 2016
- Received The Economic Times Business Leader of the Year Award in 2014
- Received CNN-IBN Indian of the Year in Business Award in 2011
- Awarded Ernst & Young (EY) Entrepreneur of the Year in 2010

KEY STRATEGIES AND SUCCESS FACTORS

Acquisitions: Acquisitions were an integral part of Sun Pharma's initial growth and continue to be the driving force of its expansion plans. Through strategic acquisitions both in India and overseas, the company was able to increase its scale rapidly and plug gaps in its product portfolio.

Focus on Global Market: Very early on, Dilip Shangvi realised that a higher life expectancy in developed countries will unlock massive potential for the pharmaceutical sector. Therefore, he expanded Sun Pharma to developed markets by investing in marketing, branding, and sales, especially in key geographies of North America and Europe. Today, Sun Pharma has a presence in over 80 countries.

Targeting Chronic Therapeutic Areas: Dilip Shanghvi has sought to focus Sun Pharma on niche, high-margin chronic therapeutic areas like psychiatry, neurology, cardiology, gastroenterology, and ophthalmology.

MALLIKA **SRINIVASAN**

Who is **Mallika Srinivasan?**

Mallika Srinivasan was born on 19th November, 1959 in Tamil Nadu into a business family. Her father A. Sivasailam, headed the Amalgamations Group of Industries. The group is involved in engineering (including auto-related manufacturing), plantations, trading & distribution, and services. Mallika obtained a degree in mathematics and then pursued her MA (Econometrics), topping the University of Madras. She went on to obtain an MBA from the prestigious Wharton School of Business.

Mallika joined the family business as General Manager, Tractors and Farm Equipment Ltd (TAFE) in 1986. At the time, TAFE's revenue was only INR 850 million. After understanding the business well, she played a key role in transforming TAFE tractors from a technology perspective, thus enhancing acceptance by farmers. Over her career, Mallika has established TAFE as a quality mass-manufacturer of tractors and agricultural equipment. She also helped drive inorganic growth at TAFE, acquiring Eicher Motors Ltd's tractor business in 2005. Mallika also expanded TAFE globally, partnering mostly with American agricultural equipment companies. TAFE has a presence in over 100 countries. Today, the company is the world's third largest manufacturer of tractors and the second largest in India, by volume. TAFE's revenues are over US$ 1.5 billion.

Besides her role as Chairman & Managing Director of TAFE, Mallika is also known for her major contributions to the agricultural machinery sector and also for her philanthropic pursuits.

Forbes estimates the net worth of Mallika Srinivasan and the Amalgamations family to be US$ 2.8 billion.

AWARDS AND RECOGNITION

- Mallika Srinivasan received India's fourth highest civilian award, the Padma Shri in 2014
- Received the US-India Business Council (USIBC) Global Leadership Award in 2021
- Conferred the Sir Jehangir Ghandy Medal by XLRI - Xavier School of Management in 2015
- Was awarded Ernst and Young (EY) Entrepreneur of the Year - Manufacturing in 2011
- Received the Woman Leader of the Year Award at the Forbes India Leadership Awards in 2012
- Named Businesswoman of the Year by The Economic Times in 2005
- Received the National Leadership Award from IIM Lucknow in 2005

KEY STRATEGIES AND
SUCCESS FACTORS

Customer Centricity: Mallika Srivasan's success is attributed to her ability to consistently drive product development on the basis of the specific requirements of Indian farmers and the conditions of Indian farms. Indian farms are typically much smaller than those overseas and hence mechanization is a challenge. TAFE has succeeded by developing sub-100 horsepower tractors that cater specifically to smaller farmers in terms of acreage.

Research & Development: One of Mallika Srinivasan's key beliefs is the importance of research & development (R&D). She has focused on continuing R&D investments in both good and bad times. She believes this allows TAFE to introduce new tractors models each year, with improved fuel efficiency, better ergonomics, and lower cost of ownership.

Strategic Partnerships and Acquisitions: A large part of TAFE's growth has been driven by partnerships and acquisitions. Most prominent was TAFE's acquisition of Eicher Motors Ltd's tractor division in 2005 for US$ 71 million. This was considered a risky acquisition because of the poor conditions in the agricultural sector. However, Mallika Srinivasan's move proved to be visionary allowing TAFE to enter the lower horsepower segment and catapulted the company into the second position in India's tractor market. In 2014, TAFE also acquired an equity stake in US headquartered Agco Corp, its long-term strategic partner.

JRD **TATA**

Who is **JRD Tata?**

JRD Tata was born in 1904 in Paris, France to a French mother and Indian father RD Tata who was a business partner and cousin of Jamsetji Tata, founder of the Tata Group. JRD was educated in France, England, and Japan and then joined the French Army for his mandatory one-year military service. He wanted to extend his military stint but his father rejected the idea. He also wanted to study engineering at Cambridge but was called back by his father to India to join the family business. In 1925, aged 21, JRD joined Tata Sons as an unpaid apprentice in an unfamiliar country. His father died in 1926 and JRD took his place as a director of Tata Sons.

In 1929, JRD gave up his French citizenship to embrace his Indian heritage and in the very same year became India's first licensed pilot. JRD founded the Tata Air Mail Service in 1932 connecting Karachi, Mumbai, Ahmedabad, and Chennai.

JRD took charge as Chairman of Tata Sons in 1938; he was only 34 and the youngest member of the Board. Soon, the air mail service was rebranded as Tata Airlines which went on to be renamed as Air India in 1946. Unfortunately, the airline was nationalized by the Government in 1953, but JRD remained Chairman till 1978.

He was Chairman of Tata Sons for nearly 60 years and strengthened the steel, power, and hospitality businesses while diversifying into chemicals, automobiles, pharmaceuticals, retail, telecom, financial services, and information technology.

Deeply committed to philanthropy, JRD helped set up several institutions to promote scientific, medical and cultural advancement in India, including the Tata Institute of Fundamental Research, Tata Memorial Hospital, the Tata Institute of Social Sciences, the National Institute of Advanced Sciences, and the National Centre for the Performing Arts.

As a result of JRD's efforts, there is almost no aspect of an Indian's life that is not touched by the Tata Group.

AWARDS AND RECOGNITION

- JRD Tata received India's highest civilian honour, the Bharat Ratna in 1992
- Was awarded India's second highest civilian award Padma Vibhushan in 1957
- Received the David Guggenheim Medal for Aviation in 1988
- Received the United Nations Population Award in 1992
- Held Honorary Air Vice Marshal rank in the Indian Air Force
- Received the French Legion of Honour Award in 1983.

KEY STRATEGIES AND
SUCCESS FACTORS

Diversification: Under JRD's leadership, the Tata Group diversified into chemicals, automobiles, pharmaceuticals, retail, telecom, financial services and IT, not to mention its foray into aviation. When JRD took over the Chairmanship of Tata Sons, its assets were about US$100 million across 14 enterprises. When he relinquished office in 1991, the Tata Group's assets had grown to $5 billion spanning 95 enterprises.

Professionalizing Management: JRD brought in brilliant business leaders and eminent intellectuals to manage the Tata Group. Over the years, JRD's leaders included giants like Russi Mody at Tata Steel, Darbari Seth at Tata Chemicals, Sumant Moolgaonkar at Tata Motors, Ajit Kerkar at Indian Hotels, FC Kohli at TCS, the legal luminary Nani Palkhivala, Dr. John Matthai, AD Shroff, Sir Ardeshir Vakil and many others.

Empathy for Employees: JRD was renowned as the 'people's man.' He was known to answer every single letter written to him by Tata employees. JRD also set up practices and systems to represent the voice of his employees; for example, 'joint works councils' were set up and these resulted in a very peaceful industrial environment in the Tata Group.

RATAN TATA

Who is **Ratan Tata?**

Ratan Tata was born on 28th December, 1937 in Mumbai into the renowned Tata family, known for both its philanthropy and its contribution to industry in India. After completing his schooling, he went on to study at Cornell University from where he obtained a bachelor's degree in architecture in 1962. Ratan worked briefly with the architecture firm Jones & Emmons in Los Angeles. He returned to India in late 1962 due to his grandmother's ill health, and landed a job at IBM. However, his mentor JRD Tata told Ratan to join the Tata Group and he did so in 1962. He later completed the Advanced Management Programme (AMP) at the Harvard Business School in 1975.

Early on, he gained experience in a variety of Tata businesses including Tata Motors and Tata Steel. In 1969, he was appointed as the Tata Group's resident representative in Australia. He returned to India in 1970, joining Tata Consultancy Services (TCS) for a short stint. He was put in charge of NELCO in 1971 and helped revive the struggling electronics company. He was then appointed to the board of Tata Sons, the Tata Group's principal holding company, in 1974. Having accumulated a lot of experience, Ratan was promoted to the Chairman of Tata Industries in 1981. He went on to draft the Tata Strategic Plan in 1983 which clearly made the case for the Group's expansion into hi-tech businesses like telecom, infotech, biotechnology, and alternative energies, etc. Between 1986-1989, he served as the Chairman of Air India, the country's national carrier.

In 1991, Ratan succeeded JRD Tata as Chairman of Tata Sons and Chairman of the Tata Trusts. During JRD Tata's time, the Group ran as a loosely controlled federation, with individual company heads having tremendous freedom, resulting in overlapping businesses and inefficiency at the Group level. Though he faced a lot of resistance, Ratan reorganized the Tata Group, exited unrelated businesses and streamlined overlapping ones, to prepare the Group for globalization. He made individual companies report operationally to the Group office and ensured that they contributed part of their profit to build and use the Tata brand. A retirement age was introduced so that older leaders made way for younger talent who would drive innovation.

Ratan Tata took the inorganic route to grow the Group globally and made several marquee acquisitions including Tetley, Corus, Jaguar Land Rover, Brunner Mond, General Chemical, and Daewoo Commercial Vehicles. During his 21 year tenure as Chairman, the Group's revenue grew 40 times and profits increased 50 fold. In 2012, Ratan stepped down as Chairman after completing 50 years with the Group, and was appointed as its Chairman Emeritus. He remains Chairman of Tata Trusts which hold 66 percent of Tata Sons.

KEY STRATEGIES AND SUCCESS FACTORS

Trust, Empowerment, and Ethics: Ratan Tata laid an emphasis on trusting employees and empowering them. This has created a culture of ownership and innovation at the Tata Group. Another powerful pillar of his leadership style is an uncompromising attitude to ethics and integrity.

Strategic Acquisitions for Global Expansion: Ratan Tata's strategic acquisitions of Tetley, Corus, Jaguar Land Rover, General Chemical, Brunner Mond, and Daewoo Commercial Vehicles, helped expand the Group's portfolio internationally. Thanks to this expansion, more than two-thirds of the Tata Group's revenue comes from international operations.

Focus on the Greater Good: Ratan Tata has continued the Tata Group's focus on philanthropy. 66 percent of Tata Sons is owned by Tata Trusts, of which Ratan Tata is Chairman. Dividends from the Tata Group are ploughed into causes such as healthcare and education by Tata Trusts. This emphasis on philanthropy and the greater good has resulted in Tata being recognized consistently as India's most trusted brand.

AWARDS AND RECOGNITION

- Ratan Tata was awarded India's second highest civilian award, the Padma Vibhushan in 2008
- Received India's third highest civilian award, the Padma Bhushan in 2000
- Was the first-ever recipient of the Udyog Ratna Award instituted by the Maharashtra Government in 2023
- Received the Carnegie Medal of Philanthropy in 2007
- Received the Ernst & Young (EY) Entrepreneur of the Year Award in 2000
- Conferred the KBE by Queen Elizabeth II of the UK in 2014
- Awarded Grand Officer of the Order of Merit of the Italian Republic in 2009
- Received the Legend in Leadership from Yale University in 2010
- Awarded Grand Cordon of the Order of the Rising Sun by the Government of Japan in 2012
- Received the Lifetime Achievement Award from the Rockefeller Foundation
- Bestowed the Lifetime Achievement Award at the Ernst & Young (EY) Awards in 2013
- Appointed Commander of the Legion of Honour by the Government of France in 2016
- Conferred Australia's highest civilian award, the Order of Australia in 2023
- Received Harvard Business School's highest honor, the Alumni Achievement Award in 1995

ACKNOWLEDGEMENTS

This book owes its origins to IBMYP Personal Project that I undertook in my tenth grade at Oberoi International School (OIS), Mumbai. Entrepreneurship, wealth creation, and history fascinate me, and this book is a celebration of all three!

While I love writing, it is an understatement to say that I am terrible at layouts and drawing. This book would have remained just a bland, printed manuscript had it not been for the designing done by Nishka Manghnani, an OIS alum. I would like to thank Chandan Naik for perfectly laying out this manuscript.

While conceptualizing this book, I wanted to make sure that it appeals to school students and young people. I wanted to add the pictures of the individuals featured in the publication. I saw photographs of serious adults in their business attire and wondered whether it would put off younger readers. Hence, the decision to introduce caricatures of the featured individuals, rather than just photographs. Gurudayal Pancheshwar is an award winning caricaturist who did all the lifelike digital caricatures for this publication. I am grateful to him.

Thanks are also due to the Notion Press publishing team who have made this book a reality.

Last but not the least, my mom Dimple, dad Kaushal and brother Dhruv. Thank you for supporting this journey. What was supposed to be a simple school project has become an obsession. This book would not have seen the light of day without your constant support, feedback and love. I dedicate it to you.

ARJUN SAMPAT

REFERENCES

5paisa. (2022, December 7). Radhakishan Damani – Success Journey. 5paisa. Retrieved April 10, 2023, from https://www.5paisa.com/finschool/radhakishan-damani-success-journey/

Abhinandan, S. (2020, December 28). Ratan Tata is rich in heart. The Youth. Retrieved January 5, 2023, from http://Ratan Tata is rich in heart

Abhinandhinee. (2022, April 11). G.D. Birla | The success story of the Indian industrialist and businessman. Failure Before Success. Retrieved January 12, 2023, from https://failurebeforesuccess.com/g-d-birla/

Accel. (2022, September 7). Secrets to Scaling with BrowserStack's Nakul Aggarwal. Accel. Retrieved February 28, 2023, from https://www.accel.com/noteworthy/secrets-to-scaling-with-browserstacks-nakul-aggarwal

Aditya Birla. (n.d.). Awards and accolades. Aditya Birla. Retrieved April 11, 2023, from https://www.adityabirla.com/about-us/heritage/aditya-vikram-birla/awards-and-accolades

Aditya Birla Group. (n.d.). New year, new beginnings. Aditya Birla Group. Retrieved July 7, 2023, from https://www.adityabirla.com/

Aditya Birla Group. (2016, May 25). Rajashree Birla: Philanthropist par excellence. Aditya Birla Group. Retrieved April 11, 2023, from https://www.adityabirla.com/media/stories/rajashree-birla-philanthropist-par-excellence

Aditya Birla Group. (2021, April 21). Shri G. D. Birla: A visionary who transformed India. Aditya Birla Group. Retrieved January 12, 2023, from https://www.adityabirla.com/media/stories/gd-birla-a-visionary-who-transformed-india

Agarwal, M. (2016, April 29). Narayana Murthy's Ten Rules For Success. Inc42. Retrieved December 8, 2022, from https://inc42.com/resources/narayana-murthys-ten-rules-for-success/

Aggarwal, N. (2023, February 11). [Personal interview by the author].

Agrawal, P., & Kulkarni, B. (2022, June 21). The curious case study of Zerodha's blue ocean strategy. Forbes India. Retrieved July 14, 2023, from https://www.forbesindia.com/article/bharatiya-vidya-bhavan039s-spjimr/the-curious-case-study-of-zerodhas-blue-ocean-strategy/77457/1

Ajwani, D. (2015, August 6). Sanjiv Goenka steps out of his father's shadow, into the limelight. Forbes India. Retrieved July 5, 2023, from https://www.forbesindia.com/article/big-bet/sanjiv-goenka-steps-out-of-his-fathers-shadow-into-the-limelight/40801/1

Almeida, A. (2021, May 12). Uday Kotak's Success Story. Trade Brains. Retrieved January 1, 2023, from https://tradebrains.in/uday-kotak-success-story/

Almeida, A. (2023, April 21). Mukesh Ambani Success Story. Trade Brains. Retrieved July 8, 2023, from https://tradebrains.in/mukesh-ambani-success-story/

Almeida, A. (2023, October 28). Ratan Tata Success Story – Biggest Achievements & Journey! Trade Brains. Retrieved November 4, 2023, from https://tradebrains.in/ratan-tata-story/

Ambuja. (2021, November 11). How Did Nykaa Become So Successful? Ambuja. Retrieved July 13, 2023, from https://www.ambujasolvex.com/blog/how-did-nykaa-become-so-successful/

Anand, K. (2016, August 30). Rakesh Jhunjhunwala reveals market strategy: 10 takeaways from his interview. The Economic Times. Retrieved December 24, 2022, from https://economictimes.indiatimes.com/markets/stocks/news/rakesh-jhunjhunwala-reveals-market-strategy-10-takeaways-from-his-interview/articleshow/53924351.cms?from=mdr

Angel One. (2020, October 25). Rakesh Junjhunwala: A Journey From Rs 5k to USD 1.8 billion. **Angel One.** Retrieved December 24, 2022, from https://www.angelone.in/smart-money/blog/

rakesh-junjhunwala-a-journey-from-rs-5k-to-usd-18-billion/

Angel One. (2021, January 16). The Success Story Of India's Vaccine King. Angel One. Retrieved July 17, 2023, from https://www.angelone.in/smart-money/blog/sucess-story-of-india-s-vaccine-king-dr-cyrus-poonawalla/

Arakali, H. (2022, May 12). How unicorn Browserstack became a profitable $100 million Indian Saas company. Forbes India. Retrieved February 28, 2023, from https://www.forbesindia.com/article/saas-rising/how-unicorn-browserstack-became-a-profitable-100-million-indian-saas-company/76223/1

Arakali, H. (Host). (2022, May 13). Ritesh Arora and Nakul Aggarwal at BrowserStack on the ambition to become the default cloud testing infrastructure [Audio podcast episode]. In Forbes India Daily Tech Conversations. https://www.forbesindia.com/audio/forbes-india-daily-tech-conver-sation/ritesh-arora-and-nakul-aggarwal-at-browserstack-on-the-ambition-to-become-the-default-cloud-testing-infrastructure/76295

Arredondo, A. (2019, May 31). Mukesh Ambani's Global Business Strategy. Linkedin. Retrieved July 4, 2023, from https://www.linkedin.com/pulse/mukesh-ambanis-global-business-strategy-andrew-arredondo/

Arun, M. G. (2021, August 17). The legacy Adi Godrej leaves behind as he steps down from group companies. India Today. Retrieved January 9, 2023, from https://www.indiatoday.in/india-today-insight/story/the-legacy-adi-godrej-leaves-behind-as-he-steps-down-from-group-companies-1841588-2021-08-17

Baruah, A. (2020, November 4). Entrepreneurs must have a 5- year profitability plan: Narayana Murthy. Mint. Retrieved December 8, 2022, from https://www.livemint.com/news/india/entrepreneurs-must-have-a-5-year-profitability-plan-narayana-murthy-11604474163565.html

Bhajantri, B. (2022, June 18). Cyrus Poonawalla. Failures before Success. Retrieved July 17, 2023, from https://failurebeforesuccess.com/cyrus-poonawalla/

Biocon. (n.d.). Kiran Mazumdar-Shaw. Biocon. Retrieved December 26, 2022, from https://www.biocon.com/about-us/board-of-directors-biocon/kiran-mazumdar-shaw-biocon/

Biocon. (2020). Kiran Mazumdar-Shaw: Awards & Recognitions: 1982-2020 [PDF]. https://archive.biocon.com/docs/Kiran-Mazumdar-Shaw-Awards-and-Recognition-20200721.pdf

Bothra, N. (2023, June 19). I wonder why there are only a few businesses like us that are built to generate profits and not raise venture capital: Nithin Kamath. Forbes India. Retrieved July 23, 2023, from https://www.forbesindia.com/article/forbes-india-pathbreakers/i-wonder-why-there-are-only-a-few-businesses-like-us-that-are-built-to-generate-profits-and-not-raise-venture-capital-nithin-kamath/85819/1

Britannica, T. Editors of Encyclopaedia (2023, October 25). J.R.D. Tata. Encyclopedia Britannica. https://www.britannica.com/biography/J-R-D-Tata

Britannica, T. Editors of Encyclopaedia (2023, December 24). Dhirubhai Ambani. Encyclopedia Britannica. https://www.britannica.com/biography/Dhirubhai-Ambani

Buildd. (n.d.). The Nykaa Marketing Strategy. Buildd. Retrieved July 13, 2023, from https://buildd.co/marketing/nykaa-marketing-strategy

Buildd. (2022, July 20). How two IITB grads scaled BrowserStack to $4B valuation & $200M revenue! Buildd. Retrieved January 7, 2023, from https://buildd.co/product/browserstack-success-story

Bundhun, R. (2022, September 12). How India's Gautam Adani became the world's third-richest person. The National News. Retrieved October 10, 2022, from https://www.thenationalnews.com/business/2022/09/12/how-indias-gautam-adani-became-the-worlds-third-richest-person/

The Business Fame. (n.d.). The Success Story of Mukesh Ambani. The Business Fame. Retrieved July 9, 2023, from https://thebusinessfame.com/mukesh-ambani-success-story/

Business Insider India. (2022, October 18). Gautam Adani's early lesson in diamond trading – a job that he left college for. Business Insider India. Retrieved October 31, 2022, from https://www.businessinsider.in/thelife/personalities/news/gautam-adanis-early-lesson-in-diamond-trading-a-job-that-he-left-college-for/articleshow/94939907.cms

Business Maps of India. (n.d.). Adi Godrej Biography. Business Maps of India. Retrieved January 9, 2023, from https://business.mapsofindia.com/business-leaders/adi-godrej.html

Business Maps of India. (n.d.). Kalanithi Maran Biography. Business Maps of India. Retrieved April 30, 2023, from https://business.mapsofindia.com/business-leaders/kalanithi-maran.html

Business Maps of India. (n.d.). Shiv Nadar. Business Maps of India. Retrieved January 5, 2023, from https://business.mapsofindia.com/business-leaders/shiv-nadar.html

Business Maps of India. (n.d.). Uday Kotak Biography. Business Maps of India. Retrieved January 1, 2023, from https://business.mapsofindia.com/business-leaders/uday-kotak.html

Business Maps of India. (n.d.). Yusuf Khwaja Hamied Biography. Business Maps of India. Retrieved December 28, 2022, from https://business.mapsofindia.com/business-leaders/yusuf-hamied.html

Business Maps of India. (2015, June 15). Anil Agarwal Biography. Business Maps of India. Retrieved December 28, 2022, from https://business.mapsofindia.com/business-leaders/anil-agarwal.html

Business Standard. (n.d.). Rahul Bajaj. Business Standard. Retrieved July 7, 2023, from https://www.business-standard.com/about/who-is-rahul-bajaj

Business Standard. (1997, May 6). Recharging Exide. Business Standard. Retrieved January 8, 2023, from https://www.business-standard.com/article/specials/recharging-exide-197050601064_1.html

Business Standard. (2021, July 19). Shiv Nadar resigns as MD of HCL Technologies, named Chairman Emeritus. Business Standard. Retrieved January 5, 2023, from https://www.business-standard.com/article/pti-stories/shiv-nadar-named-chairman-emeritus-of-hcl-technologies-121071901121_1.html

Business Today. (2022, July 3). Sajjan Jindal. Business Today. Retrieved July 14, 2023, from https://www.businesstoday.in/latest/corporate/story/jsw-steel-to-invest-rs-10000-cr-to-increase-use-of-renewable-energy-sajjan-jindal-340131-2022-07-03

Carnegie Medal of Philanthropy. (n.d.). Ratan Tata: Redefining Philanthropy in India. Carnegie Medal of Philanthropy. Retrieved January 5, 2023, from https://www.medalofphilanthropy.org/ratan-tata-redefining-philanthropy-india/

The CEO Magazine. (n.d.). Mukesh Dhirubhai Ambani. The CEO Magazine. Retrieved July 28, 2023, from https://www.theceo.in/blogs/mukesh-ambani-biography-and-life-journey

The CEO Magazine. (2021, December 21). How Ratan Tata turned his family's business into an international empire. The CEO Magazine. Retrieved January 5, 2023, from https://www.theceomagazine.com/business/coverstory/ratan-tata/

Chatterjee, D. (2015, January 28). 40 Years ago... and now- Kumar Mangalam Birla: Buying his way to the top. Business Standard. https://www.business-standard.com/article/companies/40-years-ago-and-now-kumar-mangalam-birla-buying-his-way-to-the-top-115012800005_1.html

Chatterjee, M. (2021, October 28). Lessons Every Entrepreneur can Take from JRD Tata. My Great Learning. Retrieved November 8, 2022, from https://www.mygreatlearning.com/blog/lessons-entrepreneur-can-take-from-jrd-tata/

Chegg. (2023, September 25). Radhakishan Damani: Success Story Of DMart Owner. Chegg. Retrieved December 10, 2023, from https://www.cheggindia.com/earn-online/dmart-owner-radhakishan-damani/

CNBC TV18. (n.d.). Happy Birthday Shiv Nadar: A look at the career and achievements of HCL founder and philanthropist. CNBC TV18. Retrieved December 12, 2022, from https://www.cnbctv18.com/technology/happy-birthday-shiv-nadar-a-look-at-the-career-and-achievements-of-hcl-founder-and-philanthropist-14105082.htm

CNBC TV 18. (2022, July 14). Happy Birthday Shiv Nadar. CNBC TV 18. Retrieved January 5, 2023, from https://www.cnbctv18.com/technology/happy-birthday-shiv-nadar-a-look-at-the-career-and-achievements-of-hcl-founder-and-philanthropist-14105082.htm

Cyrus Poonawalla Group. (n.d.). Cyrus Poonawalla Group. Cyrus Poonawalla Group. Retrieved July 17, 2023, from https://www.cyruspoonawallagroup.com/

Daniel, A. (2019, December 6). INSIGHTS #43 Kiran Mazumdar Shaw shares her Biocon journey and reveals why entrepreneurs need to be risk-takers. Medium. Retrieved December 26, 2022, from https://medium.com/accel-india-insights/insights-43-kiran-mazumdar-shaw-shares-her-biocon-journey-and-reveals-why-entrepreneurs-need-to-869a9bae3ad5

Das, S. (2021, September 17). Biocon Biologics, Serum Institute Life Sciences enter strategic alliance. Business Standard. Retrieved July 17, 2023, from https://www.business-standard.com/article/companies/biocon-biologics-serum-institute-life-sciences-enter-strategic-alliance-121091700898_1.html

Datta, A. (2018, September 24). Kumar Mangalam Birla: As acquisitive as ever. Fortune India. Retrieved July 7, 2023, from https://www.fortuneindia.com/enterprise/kumar-mangalam-birla-as-acquisitive-as-ever/102494

Datta, A., & Majumdar, S. (2017, November 24). Adi Godrej: An entrepreneur and a gentleman. Forbes India. Retrieved January 9, 2023, from https://www.forbesindia.com/article/leadership-awards-2017/adi-godrej-an-entrepreneur-and-a-gentleman/48721/1

DiLallo, M. (2015, May 10). Mukesh Ambani. The Motley Fool. Retrieved July 8, 2023, from https://www.fool.com/investing/general/2015/05/10/mukesh-ambani-going-backward-to-move-forward-and-m.aspx

DNA Web Team. (2023, May 23). Meet 'Tractor Queen' Mallika Srinivasan, leads Rs 10,000 crore turnover business, her net worth is…. DNA. Retrieved July 15, 2023, from https://www.dnaindia.com/business/report-meet-tractor-queen-mallika-srinivasan-leads-rs-10000-crore-turnover-business-her-net-worth-is-tafe-3043964

Dua, G. (2022, January 20). Success Story of Sanjiv Goenka. Startup Talky. Retrieved July 5, 2023, from https://startuptalky.com/sanjiv-goenka-rpsg-group/

The Economic Times. (2015, March 9). Shiv Nadar Foundation sells shares worth Rs 1,150 crore in HCL Tech. The Economic Times. Retrieved January 5, 2023, from https://economictimes.indiatimes.com/tech/software/shiv-nadar-foundation-sells-shares-worth-rs-1150-crore-in-hcl-tech/articleshow/46503268.cms?from=mdr

The Economic Times. (2018, July 7). Mukesh Ambani gets another 5 years as Reliance Chairman. The Economic Times. Retrieved July 25, 2023, from https://economictimes.indiatimes.com/news/company/corporate-trends/mukesh-ambani-gets-another-5-years-as-reliance-chairman/articleshow/64896192.cms?from=mdr

The Economic Times. (2020, August 17). Uday Kotak. The Economic Times. Retrieved January 1, 2023, from https://economictimes.indiatimes.com/markets/expert-view/in-finance-technology-and-business-we-are-moving-to-a-never-normal-world-uday-kotak/articleshow/77585088.cms?from=mdr

The Economic Times. (2020, October 7). Rajan Raheja. The Economic Times. Retrieved January 1, 2023, from https://economictimes.indiatimes.com/panache/panache-people-101/rajan-raheja/profileshow/81707420.cms

The Economic Times. (2022, February 14). Rahul Bajaj: Man who called a spade a spade even if it meant ruffling feathers in the government. The Economic Times. Retrieved July 5, 2023, from https://economictimes.indiatimes.com/news/company/corporate-trends/rahul-bajaj-man-who-called-spade-a-spade-even-it-meant-ruffling-feathers-in-government/articleshow/89530529.cms?from=mdr

Entrepreneur India. (2019, December 28). Kiran Mazumdar Shaw and Lessons In Entrepreneurship. Entrepreneur India. Retrieved December 26, 2022, from https://www.entrepreneur.com/en-in/entrepreneurs/kiran-mazumdar-shaw-and-lessons-in-entrepreneurship/344346

Essar. (n.d.). Essar Group. Essar. Retrieved January 1, 2023, from https://www.essar.com/

Essar. (n.d.). Ravi Ruia. https://www.essar.com/about/ravi-ruia/. Retrieved December 5, 2023, from https://www.essar.com/about/ravi-ruia/

Essar. (n.d.). Shashi Ruia. Essar. Retrieved December 5, 2023, from https://www.essar.com/about/shashi-ruia/

ET Bureau. (2011, August 9). 30 lessons from life and career of NR Narayana Murthy. Economic Times. Retrieved December 8, 2022, from https://economictimes.indiatimes.com/management-leaders/30-lessons-from-life-and-career-of-nr-narayana-murthy/slideshow/9656278.cms

ET Bureau. (2012, October 23). ET Awards 2012. The Economic Times. Retrieved July 7, 2023, from https://economictimes.indiatimes.com/news/company/corporate-trends/et-awards-2012-aditya-birla-group-bags-the-corporate-citizen-of-the-year-award/articleshow/16457744.cms?from=mdr

ET Bureau. (2022, February 12). Rahul Bajaj: Remembering the storied legacy of a true trailblazer. The Economic Times. Retrieved July 5, 2023, from https://economictimes.indiatimes.com/news/company/corporate-trends/rahul-bajaj-the-legacy-of-a-trailblazer/articleshow/89532101.cms

ET Now Digital. (2020, August 9). Throwback: When Infosys founder Narayana Murthy was jailed for 3 days without food in Bulgaria. Times Now News. Retrieved December 8, 2022, from https://www.timesnownews.com/business-economy/companies/article/throwback-when-infosys-founder-narayana-murthy-was-jailed-for-3-days-without-food-in-bulgaria/634102

Faber. (2020, July 11). Entrepreneur Anil Agarwal Success Story - Chairman Of Vedanta Group. VTV India. Retrieved December 28, 2022, from https://www.vtvindia.com/Anil-Agarwal-Success-Story

Financial Express. (2023, April 29). Kumar Mangalam Birla. Financial Express. Retrieved July 6, 2023, from https://www.financialexpress.com/lifestyle/kumar-mangalam-birla-the-inspiring-journey-of-one-of-indias-most-prominent-businessmen-know-about-his-life-net-worth-more/3043635/

Forbes. (2011, November 23). Ploughshares To Profits. Forbes. Retrieved July 7, 2023, from https://www.forbes.com/global/2011/1205/asia-power-business-women-mallika-srinivasan-tafe-ploughshares-raghunathan.html?sh=4987b8a65cf5

Forbes. (2012, June 22). Indian Billionaire Shiv Nadar's Education Plan. Forbes. Retrieved January 5, 2023, from https://www.forbes.com/global/2011/0718/heroes-philanthropy-11-shiv-nadar-vidyagyan-getting-them-young.html?sh=5c0d82c325e9

The Global Hues. (2021, June 29). The Success Story Of Gautam Adani: Ambitions Turn To Reality. The Global Hues. Retrieved October 31, 2022, from https://theglobalhues.com/the-success-story-of-gautam-adani-ambitions-turn-to-reality/

Godrej. (2019). Annual & Integrated Report 2018-2019. Godrej. Retrieved January 9, 2023, from https://www.godrejcp.com/annual-reports/2018-19/strategic-pillars/accelerating-innovation-and-building-purposeful-brands/

Gopinath, V. (2018, June 11). GD Birla: A Gandhian Who Rose With the Fall of the British. The Quint. Retrieved January 12, 2023, from https://www.thequint.com/news/politics/ghanshyam-das-birla-mahatma-gandhi-friendship-relationship#read-more

Goyal, S. (2022, August 24). Gautam Adani Biography. Jagran Josh. Retrieved January 3, 2024, from https://www.jagranjosh.com/general-knowledge/gautam-adani-biography-1642144168-1

Guru, S. (2015, October 1). Remembering Aditya Birla. Aditya Birla. Retrieved April 11, 2023, from https://www.adityabirla.com/media/press-reports/remembering-aditya-birla

Hamied, Y. (2017, July 25). Doctor Yusuf K. Hamied on the importance of public-funded research being free for the public. Humans of Science. Retrieved December 28, 2022, from https://www.humans-of-science.org/single-post/2017/07/25/Dr-Yusuf-Hamied-on-the-importance-of-public-funded-research-being-free-for-the-public

Harvard Business School. (n.d.). Rahul Bajaj. Harvard Business School. Retrieved July 5, 2023, from https://www.hbs.edu/creating-emerging-markets/interviews/Pages/profile.aspx?profile=rbajaj

Hazarika, S. (1995, October 3). Aditya Vikram Birla, 51, A Leading Indian Businessman. The New York Times. Retrieved April 11, 2023, from https://www.nytimes.com/1995/10/03/business/aditya-vikram-birla-51-a-leading-indian-businessman.html

HCL Tech. (2022). HCL Technologies Report 2022. HCL Tech. Retrieved December 12, 2022, from https://www.hcltech.com/hcl-annual-report-2022/Business-highlights-engineering.php

Hollar, S. (2023, August 16). Narayana Murthy. Encyclopedia Britannica. https://www.britannica.com/biography/Narayana-Murthy

Hollar, S. (2023, December 9). Kiran Mazumdar-Shaw. Encyclopedia Britannica. https://www.britannica.com/biography/Kiran-Mazumdar-Shaw

Hollar, S. (2023, December 24). Ratan Tata. Encyclopedia Britannica. https://www.britannica.com/biography/Ratan-Tata

I Love India. (n.d.). Aditya Vikram Birla. I Love India. Retrieved April 11, 2023, from https://www.iloveindia.com/indian-heroes/aditya-vikram-birla.html

India CSR. (2017, August 4). Reliance Foundation spends Rs 3150 Cr in last five years. India CSR. Retrieved July 4, 2023, from https://indiacsr.in/reliance-foundation-spends-rs-3150-cr-in-last-five-years/#:~:text=MUMBAI%3A%20Reliance%20Foundation%2C%20CSR%20arm%20of%20Reliance%20Industries,law%20for%20CSR%2C%20it%20said%20in%20a%20statement.

Indian Bill gate. (2022). Aditya Vikram Birla-Former Chairman of Aditya Birla Group. Indian Bill gate. Retrieved January 5, 2023, from https://indianbillgates.com/aditya-vikram-birla/

Iyer, R. (n.d.). Sanjiv Goenka. Leader Biography. Retrieved July 5, 2023, from https://www.leaderbiography.com/sanjiv-goenka-lucknow-super-giants-owner/

Jaiswar, P. S. (2022, August 14). 'Success is temporary' A journey of Rakesh Jhunjhunwala's net worth from 1cr to over 46000cr. Mint. Retrieved December 24, 2022, from https://www.livemint.com/market/stock-market-news/-success-is-temporary-a-journey-of-rakesh-jhunjhunwala-s-net-worth-from-rs-1-cr-to-over-rs-46-000-cr-11660477911487.htmlhttps://www.livemint.com/market/stock-market-news/-success-is-temporary-a-journey-of-rakesh-jhunjhunwala-s-net-worth-from-rs-1-cr-to-over-rs-46-000-cr-11660477911487.html

Javaid, A. (2022, December 28). Ratan Tata Biography. Jagran Josh. Retrieved January 5, 2023, from https://www.jagranjosh.com/general-knowledge/ratan-tata-biography-1640668054-1

Jayaram, A. (2022, September 12). Birla, The Commodity King. The Fortune India. Retrieved January 5, 2023, from https://www.fortuneindia.com/long-reads/birla-the-commodity-king/109603

John, N. (2023, April 10). JSW Group: Life Beyond Steel. Fortune India. Retrieved July 14, 2023, from https://www.fortuneindia.com/long-reads/jsw-group-life-beyond-steel/112193

Josh, J. (2022, August 24). Radhakishan Damani Biography. Jagran Josh. Retrieved July 7, 2023, from https://www.jagranjosh.com/general-knowledge/radhakishan-damani-biography-early-life-career-investments-current-position-recent-news-and-more-1661358338-1

JSW Foundation. (n.d.). Building Communities. Transforming Lives. JSW Foundation. Retrieved July 13, 2023, from https://www.jsw.in/foundation/about-jsw-foundation-0

Kalesh, B. (2014, January 13). How a forced split of RPG enterprises actually worked for Goenka brothers. The Economic Times. Retrieved July 2, 2023, from https://economictimes.indiatimes.com/news/company/corporate-trends/how-a-forced-split-of-rpg-enterprises-actually-worked-for-goenka-brothers/articleshow/28720838.cms?from=mdr

Kamath, G. (2012, January 19). Don't look now, Cipla just might be changing, says Cipla chairman & MD Dr Yusuf Hamied. The Economic Times. Retrieved December 28, 2022, from https://economictimes.indiatimes.com/industry/healthcare/biotech/pharmaceuticals/dont-look-now-cipla-just-might-be-changing-says-cipla-chairman-md-dr-yusuf-hamied/articleshow/11547741.cms?from=mdr

Kant, K., & Divekar, A. (2015, February 9). Sajjan Jindal: Cautiously opportunistic. Business Standard. Retrieved July 17, 2023, from https://www.business-standard.com/article/companies/sajjan-jindal-cautiously-opportunistic-115020901033_1.html

Karan. (2015, July 15). Kalanithi Maran. Yo Success. Retrieved April 30, 2023, from https://www.yosuccess.com/success-stories/kalanithi-maran-sun-group/

Kaur, S. (2020, December 2). What marketing strategy makes Nykaa so unique? The Strategy Story. Retrieved July 13, 2023, from https://thestrategystory.com/2020/12/02/beauty-e-commerce-startup-nykaa-marketing-strategy/

Kay, C., & R, S. P. (2022, September 28). A Hostile Media Bid Shows How Asia's Richest Men Can Align and Dominate a Sector. Bloomberg. Retrieved July 22, 2023, from https://www.bloomberg.com/news/articles/2022-09-27/hostile-ndtv-bid-shows-gautam-adani-mukesh-ambani-are-formidable-when-aligned?leadSource=uverify%20wall

Keshadev, V. (2022, May 10). Kotak Mahindra. Fortune India. Retrieved January 1, 2023, from https://www.fortuneindia.com/long-reads/kotak-mahindra-run-fast-run-slow-repeat/108101

Khan, A. (2023, November 14). Aditya Vikram Birla. Your Story. Retrieved December 11, 2023, from https://yourstory.com/2023/11/aditya-vikram-birla-success-mantras

Kitey, V. (2021, August 4). D'Mart: Most Successful Indian Chain of Hypermarkets[DMart Case Study]. Startup Talky. Retrieved April 10, 2023, from https://startuptalky.com/dmart-case-study/

Layak, S. (2011, October 11). Will Kumar Mangalam Birla's constellation be in alignment with his goal? Business Today. Retrieved July 7, 2023, from https://www.businesstoday.in/magazine/cover-story/story/the-kumar-mangalam-birla-core-business-team-26386-2011-09-28

Layak, S. (2017, January 13). Ratan Tata wants to turn his focus to philanthropy. The Economic Times. Retrieved January 7, 2023, from https://economictimes.indiatimes.com/news/company/corporate-trends/ratan-tata-wants-to-turn-his-focus-to-philanthropy/articleshow/56507707.cms

Layak, S. (2019, April 21). How Sanjiv Goenka transformed RPSG group into a conglomerate with diverse revenue streams. The Economic Times. Retrieved July 5, 2023, from https://economictimes.indiatimes.com/industry/cons-products/fmcg/how-sanjiv-goenka-transformed-rpsg-group-into-a-conglomerate-with-diverse-revenue-streams/articleshow/68969527.cms?from=mdr

Layak, S., & Shukla, G. (2012, April 13). Acquisitions have been part of our DNA: Harsh Goenka. Business Today. Retrieved July 2, 2023, from https://www.businesstoday.in/opinion/interviews/story/harsh-goenka-rpg-enterprises-interview-31662-2012-04-12

Live Mint. (2014, September 24). Hindalco now entering consolidation phase: Kumar Mangalam Birla. Live Mint. Retrieved July 7, 2023, from https://www.livemint.com/Companies/b2zdUaSzydf8cjgKepYg2O/Hindalco-now-entering-consolidation-phase-Kumar-Mangalam-

Bi.html

Lobo, R. (n.d.). A look at the Ruia brothers' takeover of Essar Energy. World Finance. Retrieved December 5, 2023, from https://www.worldfinance.com/markets/a-look-at-the-ruia-brothers-takeover-of-essar-energy

Lodha, V. (2021, November 26). Entrepreneurship Lessons from Falguni Nayar. Linkedin. Retrieved July 13, 2023, from https://www.linkedin.com/pulse/entrepreneurship-lessons-from-falguni-nayar-vivek-lodha/

London Speaker Bureau. (2015, November 25). Harsh Mariwala. London Speaker Bureau. Retrieved January 6, 2023, from https://hi.londonspeakerbureau.com/speaker-profile/harsh-mariwala/#:~:text=Mariwala%20received%3B%20the%202009%20Ernst,HRM%20Congress%20'CEO%20with%20HR

Madhukalya, A. (2023, July 5). Nithin Kamath on the origins of Zerodha. Business Today. Retrieved July 24, 2023, from https://www.businesstoday.in/latest/corporate/story/i-quickly-realised-that-nikhil-is-a-better-trader-than-i-am-nithin-kamath-on-the-origins-of-zerodha-388279-2023-07-05

Majumdar, S. (2015, January 14). How Dhirubhai Ambani changed the style of doing business in India. Rediff. Retrieved December 22, 2022, from https://www.rediff.com/money/special/pix-special-how-dhirubhai-ambani-changed-the-idiom-of-doing-business/20150114.htm

Makhija, M. (2022, July 20). Kiran Mazumdar Shaw: How Biocon Founder Became India's First Biotech Queen? Startup Talky. Retrieved December 26, 2022, from https://startuptalky.com/kiran-mazumdar-shaw-success-story/

Manohar, A. (2022, August 14). https://www.livemint.com/market/stock-market-news/rakesh-jhunjhunwala-s-10-investment-principles-that-made-him-big-bull-of-street-11660452998708.html. Mint. Retrieved December 24, 2022, from https://www.livemint.com/market/stock-market-news/rakesh-jhunjhunwala-s-10-investment-principles-that-made-him-big-bull-of-street-11660452998708.html

Marico. (2022). Integrated Report 2021-22. Marico. Retrieved January 6, 2023, from https://marico.com/page/DigitalReport2021-2022/

Marico Innovation Foundation. (n.d.). Marico Innovation Foundation. Marico Innovation Foundation. Retrieved January 6, 2023, from https://www.maricoinnovationfoundation.org/about-us/

Mariwala, H. (2021, November 17). Why is digital a must-have for new-age Indian entrepreneurs. Entrepreneur India. Retrieved January 6, 2023, from https://www.entrepreneur.com/en-in/growth-strategies/why-is-digital-a-must-have-for-new-age-indian-entrepreneurs/397626

Mariwala, H. (2022, August 15). The Evolution of Indian Entrepreneurship. Business Line. Retrieved January 6, 2023, from https://www.thehindubusinessline.com/india-at-75/75-years-of-independence-the-evolution-of-indian-entrepreneurship/article65761573.ece

Mariwala, H. (2022, November 18). Harsh Mariwala. CNBC TV18. Retrieved January 6, 2023, from https://www.cnbctv18.com/business/marico-founder-harsh-mariwala-tips-on-entrepreneurship-owners-running-company-15195361.htm

Mariwala, H. (2023, January 11). [Personal interview by the author].

Mariwala, H., & Charan, R. (2021, August 2). How Marico fought an aggressive giant. Mint. Retrieved January 6, 2023, from https://www.livemint.com/mint-lounge/features/how-marico-fought-an-aggressive-giant-11627843467795.html

Mariwala, H., Charan, R., Mariwala, A., & Nair, J. (2021). Harsh realities: The making of Marico. Penguin Business, an imprint of Penguin Random House.

Martins, M. (2019, June 19). Nykaa to expand offline footprint, plans to open 180 stores by 2024. Fashion Network. Retrieved July 13, 2023, from https://in.fashionnetwork.com/news/Nykaa-to-expand-offline-footprint-plans-to-open-180-stores-by-2024,1110959.html

Menon, R. (2017, December 13). Sajjan Jindal. The Economic Times. Retrieved July 17, 2023, from https://economictimes.indiatimes.com/magazines/panache/in-1984-i-was-newly-married-had-no-money-and-hated-borrowing-from-my-dad-sajjan-jindal/articleshow/62048140.cms

Mint. (2022, September 16). Adani Group now the 2nd largest cement play as acquisition of Ambuja Cements, ACC completes. Mint. Retrieved October 31, 2022, from https://www.livemint.com/companies/news/adani-group-now-the-2nd-largest-cement-player-as-acquisition-of-ambuja-cements-acc-completes-11663329343722.html

Mishra, A. K. (2013, November 12). Rahul Bajaj: 'I Am No Saint'. Forbes India. Retrieved July 5, 2023, from https://www.forbesindia.com/article/india-rich-list-2013/rahul-bajaj-i-am-no-saint/36501/1

Mukherjee, U. (2019, July 12). Kumar Mangalam Birla consolidates group companies under BGH. Times of India. Retrieved July 6, 2023, from https://timesofindia.indiatimes.com/business/india-business/k-m-birla-consolidates-group-cos-under-bgh/articleshow/70184509.cms

Narang, P. (n.d.). Radhakishan Damani, The Indian Billionaire Investor Behind DMart. The CEO Magazine. Retrieved July 7, 2023, from https://www.theceo.in/top-ceo-profiles/radhakishan-damani-the-indian-billionaire-investor-behind-dmart

Narayanan, S. (2021, January 11). India's digital-first banker. Stratergy-Business. Retrieved January 1, 2023, from https://www.strategy-business.com/article/Indias-digital-first-banker

News 18. (2022, August 18). Radhakrishna Damani's DMart Eyes Five Fold Expansion. News 18. Retrieved April 5, 2023, from https://www.news18.com/news/business/radhakrishna-damanis-dmart-eyes-five-fold-expansion-know-details-5774467.html

Nolen, J. L. (2024, January 3). Mukesh Ambani. Encyclopedia Britannica. https://www.britannica.com/biography/Mukesh-Ambani

Padhnis, S. (2021, July 20). Shiv Nadar ends his innings at HCL. The Times of India. Retrieved January 5, 2023, from Shiv Nadar ends his innings at HCL Read more at: http://timesofindia.indiatimes.com/articleshow/84576727.cms?utm_source=contentofinterest&utm_medium=text&utm_campaign=cppst

Pai, A. (2021, March 6). Reliance Industries: Moving forward with backward integration. The Strategy Story. Retrieved December 22, 2022, from https://thestrategystory.com/2021/03/06/reliance-backward-integration/

Paul, C. (2015, January 17). How Kalanithi Maran lost SpiceJet. Forbes India. Retrieved April 30, 2023, from https://www.forbesindia.com/article/boardroom/how-kalanithi-maran-lost-spicejet/39401/1

People Pill. (n.d.). Harsh Goenka. People Pill. Retrieved July 2, 2023, from https://peoplepill.com/i/harsh-goenka

People Pill. (n.d.). Sajjan Jindal. People Pill. Retrieved July 17, 2023, from https://peoplepill.com/i/sajjan-jindal

Poddar, N. (2021, October 26). Customer acquisition is near-term focus, not maximising profitability: Falguni Nayar, Nykaa. Money Control. Retrieved July 13, 2023, from https://www.moneycontrol.com/news/business/customer-acquisition-is-near-term-focus-and-not-maximising-profitability-falguni-nayar-nykaa-7625741.html

Prasad, R. (2013, March 11). RPG Enterprises chairman Harsh Goenka plans a complete makeover. The Economic Times. Retrieved July 2, 2023, from https://economictimes.indiatimes.com/news/company/corporate-trends/rpg-enterprises-chairman-harsh-goenka-plans-a-complete-makeover/articleshow/18903917.cms?from=mdr

R, S. P. (2022, November 22). Essar Group Completes Asset Sales to Become Debt Free. Bloomberg.

Retrieved December 5, 2023, from https://www.bloomberg.com/news/articles/2022-11-21/essar-group-completes-asset-sales-to-become-debt-free

Rajan, M. C. (2012, October 26). Rise and rise of media moghuls Dayanidhi and Kalanithi Maran. India Today. Retrieved April 30, 2023, from https://www.indiatoday.in/india/south/story/rise-of-media-moghuls-sun-tv-owner-dayanidhi-maran-kalanithi-marans-119637-2012-10-25

Raje, A. P. (2014, April 6). Harsh Mariwala: The inside-out thinker. Live Mint. Retrieved January 6, 2023, from https://www.livemint.com/Leisure/XuWGTODJjudf5DUNGyQLcN/Harsh-Mariwala--The-insideout-thinker.html

Ramnath, N. S. (2012, October 11). Tafe, Mallika Srinivasan: The Tractor Queen. Forbes India. Retrieved July 7, 2023, from https://www.forbesindia.com/article/leaderhip-awards-2012/tafe-mallika-srinivasan-the-tractor-queen/33883/1

Rao, D. (2022, June 9). Unicorn-Entrepreneurship. Forbes. Retrieved July 13, 2023, from https://www.forbes.com/sites/dileeprao/2022/06/09/unicorn-entrepreneurship-5-finance-smart-secrets-from-falguni-nayar-of-nykaa/?sh=22710e632383

Ray, S. S. (2022, April 28). JSPL to increase production capacity fivefold to 50 mtpa. Financial Express. Retrieved July 13, 2022, from https://www.financialexpress.com/business/industry-jspl-to-increase-production-capacity-fivefold-to-50-mtpa-2505937/

Rediff. (2004, August 19). JRD Tata: A life extraordinary. Rediff. Retrieved November 8, 2022, from https://www.rediff.com/money/2004/aug/19tata.htm

Rediff. (2005, February 16). 'Don't be too smart, looking foolish is OK'. Rediff. Retrieved December 28, 2022, from https://www.rediff.com/money/2005/feb/16inter.htm

Reliance Industry Limited. (n.d.). Growth is Life. Reliance Industry Limited. Retrieved July 8, 2023, from https://www.ril.com/

Robertson, C. (2021, February 28). Covid: How this Indian firm is vaccinating the world. BBC. Retrieved June 17, 2023, from https://www.bbc.com/news/business-56218058

S, R. (n.d.). RP Sanjiv Goenka's CESC splits into four companies. Business Line. Retrieved July 5, 2023, from https://www.thehindubusinessline.com/companies/rp-sanjiv-goenkas-cesc-splits-into-four-companies/article9706994.ece

SAI University. (n.d.). N. R. Narayana Murthy. SAI University. Retrieved December 8, 2022, from https://saiuniversity.edu.in/team/nr-narayana-murthy/

Seth, D., & Tripathi, S. (2021, December 26). MPW: How Falguni Nayar Led Nykaa to a Successful IPO. Business Today. Retrieved July 13, 2023, from https://www.businesstoday.in/specials/most-powerful-women-in-business/story/mpw-how-falguni-nayar-led-nykaa-to-a-successful-ipo-315192-2021-12-10

Sharma, A. (2010, August 10). India's Other Rich Brothers Aim High. Wall Street Journal. Retrieved December 5, 2023, from https://www.wsj.com/articles/SB10001424052748704741904575409010589856580

Sharma, D. (2021, September 24). Yusuf Hamied: The Global Celebrity of Pharmaceuticals and Non-Executive Chairman of Cipla. Read more at: https://thedigitalyug.com/stories/yusuf-hamied-the-global-celebrity-of-pharmaceuticals-and-non-executive-chairman-of-cipla. Digital Yug. Retrieved December 28, 2022, from https://thedigitalyug.com/stories/yusuf-hamied-the-global-celebrity-of-pharmaceuticals-and-non-executive-chairman-of-cipla

Sharma, K. (2022, May 24). The success story of Cyrus Poonawalla. Business Insider India. Retrieved January 1, 2023, from https://www.businessinsider.in/business/news/how-cyrus-poonawalla-became-one-of-the-worlds-richest-billionaires/articleshow/91763784.cms

Shiv Nadar Biography. (n.d.). Business Maps of India. Retrieved December 12, 2022, from https://business.mapsofindia.com/business-leaders/shiv-nadar.htmlShiv Nadar Biography

Shiv Nadar Foundation. (n.d.). Shiv Nadar Foundation. Shiv Nadar Foundation. Retrieved January

5, 2023, from https://www.shivnadarfoundation.org/

Shiv Nadar Foundation. (n.d.). Shiv Nadar Foundation. Shiv Nadar Foundation. Retrieved December 12, 2022, from https://www.shivnadarfoundation.org/

Shridhar, J. (2022, February 28). Remembering Rahul Bajaj: An exceptional business leader, independent and forthright. Financial Express. Retrieved July 5, 2023, from https://www.financialexpress.com/opinion/remembering-rahul-bajaj-an-exceptional-business-leader-independent-and-forthright/2446757/

Shyam, A. (2016, November 18). New Models, normal rains lift M&M tractor growth. The Economic Times. Retrieved July 7, 2023, from https://economictimes.indiatimes.com/markets/stocks/news/new-models-normal-rains-lift-mm-tractor-growth/articleshow/55488533.cms?from=mdr

Singh, S. (2015, November 14). How Shiv Nadar Foundation is making its impact on society. The Economic Times. Retrieved January 5, 2023, from https://economictimes.indiatimes.com/news/company/corporate-trends/how-shiv-nadar-foundation-is-making-its-impact-on-the-society/articleshow/49751191.cms

Soni, Y., & Babu, V. (2023, May 8). The billionaire brokers. The Hindu Business Line. Retrieved July 23, 2023, from https://www.thehindubusinessline.com/blchangemakers/the-billionaire-brokers/article65865885.ece

Srivastava, S. (2015, October 20). Harsh Goenka and CEAT: Getting a stronger grip. Forbes India. Retrieved July 2, 2023, from https://www.forbesindia.com/article/india-rich-list-2015/harsh-goenka-and-ceat-getting-a-stronger-grip/41285/1

Stars Unfolded. (n.d.). Kalanithi Maran. Stars Unfolded. Retrieved April 30, 2023, from https://starsunfolded.com/kalanithi-maran/

Starsunfolded. (n.d.). kiran Mazumdar. Starsunfolded. Retrieved December 26, 2022, from https://starsunfolded.com/kiran-mazumdar/

Starsunfolded. (n.d.). N. R. Narayana Murthy. Starsunfolded. Retrieved December 8, 2022, from https://starsunfolded.com/n-r-narayana-murthy/

Stars Unfolded. (n.d.). Shiv Nadar. Stars Unfolded. Retrieved January 5, 2023, from https://starsunfolded.com/shiv-nadar/

Success Story. (n.d.). Kalanithi Maran Success Story. Success Story. Retrieved April 30, 2923, from https://successstory.com/people/kalanithi-maran

Success Story. (n.d.). Rajan Raheja Story. Success Story. Retrieved January 8, 2023, from https://successstory.com/people/rajan-biharilal-raheja-1471

Sugar Mint. (n.d.). DMart's Radhakishan Damani Inspiring Success Story. Sugar Mint. Retrieved July 7, 2023, from https://sugermint.com/dmarts-radhakishan-damani-inspiring-success-story/

Sugar Mint. (n.d.). Uday Kotak. Sugar Mint. Retrieved January 1, 2023, from https://sugermint.com/uday-kotak-success-story-man-behind-kotak-mahindra-bank/

Surendar, T. (2007, December 15). 'You have to learn new skills in business'. The Times of India. Retrieved December 5, 2023, from https://timesofindia.indiatimes.com/business/india-business/you-have-to-learn-new-skills-in-business/articleshow/2623487.cms?from=mdr

Talkhedkar, A. (2021, December 5). Lesser-known and interesting facts about Rajan Raheja. Business Upturn. Retrieved January 8, 2023, from https://www.businessupturn.com/features/lesser-known-and-interesting-facts-about-rajan-raheja/

Tandon, T. (2022, August 16). Rakesh Jhunjhunwala Biography. Jagran Josh. Retrieved December 24, 2022, from https://www.jagranjosh.com/general-knowledge/rakesh-jhunjhunwala-biography-portfolio-net-worth-investments-age-house-wife-1654512763-1

Tata. (n.d.). Ratan Naval Tata. Tata. Retrieved January 5, 2023, from https://www.tata.com/

about-us/tata-group-our-heritage/tata-titans/ratan-naval-tata

Tata Group. (n.d.). Jehangir Ratanji Dadabhoy Tata. Tata Group. Retrieved November 8, 2022, from https://www.tata.com/about-us/tata-group-our-heritage/tata-titans/jrd-tata

TeamTGH. (2020, December 8). Biography of Kiran Mazumdar Shaw. The Global Hues. Retrieved December 26, 2022, from https://theglobalhues.com/biography-kiran-mazumdar-shaw/

Tech Gig. (2022, June 28). 5 Key learnings and takeaways from HCL founder Shiv Nadar. Tech Gig. Retrieved January 5, 2023, from https://content.techgig.com/leadership/5-key-learnings-and-takeaways-from-hcl-founder-shiv-nadar/articleshow/92520355.cms

TechGig Bureau. (2022, June 28). 5 Key learnings and takeaways from HCL founder Shiv Nadar. Tech Gig. Retrieved December 12, 2022, from https://content.techgig.com/leadership/5-key-learnings-and-takeaways-from-hcl-founder-shiv-nadar/articleshow/92520355.cms

Tiwari, A. (2021, September 5). Shiv Nadar's Legacy. India Times. Retrieved January 5, 2023, from https://www.indiatimes.com/trending/human-interest/shiv-nadar-founder-of-hcl-technologies-success-story-548745.html

Tiwari, A. (2021, September 5). Shiv Nadar's Legacy: Meet The Man Who Led HCL To Success. India Times. Retrieved December 12, 2022, from https://www.indiatimes.com/trending/human-interest/shiv-nadar-founder-of-hcl-technologies-success-story-548745.htmlShiv   Nadar's Legacy: Meet The Man Who Led HCL To Success

Tiwari, A. (2022, January 22). 15 Instances When Ratan Tata Proved That He Is A True Gem Of The Country. India Times. Retrieved January 5, 2023, from https://www.indiatimes.com/trending/human-interest/ratan-tata-man-with-golden-heart-560055.html

TMTL. (n.d.). TAFE Motors and Tractors Limited. TMTL. Retrieved July 7, 2023, from https://tmtl.in/corporate/mallika-srinivasan.php

Trade Brains. (2021, October 5). Zerodha Success Story. Trade Brains. Retrieved July 23, 2023, from https://tradebrains.in/zerodha-success-story/

T Telegana. (n.d.). Biography of Aditya Vikram Birla. T Telegana. Retrieved January 5, 2023, from https://www.ttelangana.com/biography-of-aditya-vikram-birla/

Unacademy. (n.d.). Works and Achievements of JRD Tata. Unacademy. Retrieved November 8, 2022, from https://unacademy.com/content/ssc/study-material/general-awareness/works-and-achievements-of-jrd-tata/

Varghese, C. (n.d.). The RP-Sanjiv Goenka Group. Market Feed. Retrieved July 5, 2023, from https://www.marketfeed.com/read/en/the-rp-sanjiv-goenka-group-origin-businesses

Venketakrishnan, A. (2012, April 3). Venketakrishnan. Mint. Retrieved July 7, 2023, from https://www.livemint.com/Companies/JRHSUTgB5SIbLIt1CIuNRI/Tractor-maker-Tafe-revenue-grows-30-to-add-capacity.html

Vijayraghavan, K., & Malviya, S. (2015, March 25). Radhakishan Damani: Man with the Midas touch in stock markets. The Economic Times. Retrieved July 7, 2023, from https://economictimes.indiatimes.com/radhakishan-damani-man-with-the-midas-touch-in-the-stock-markets/articleshow/32630959.cms?from=mdr

Vyshnavi, P. (2020, November 19). The Subsidiaries That Make Reliance Industries Successful. Startup Talky. Retrieved July 4, 2023, from https://startuptalky.com/subsidiaries-reliance-industries/

Wangchuk, R. N. (2022, June 8). GD Birla: The 'Nationalist Businessman' Who Helped Fund The Freedom Struggle. The Better India. Retrieved January 12, 2023, from https://www.thebetterindia.com/287887/ghanshyam-das-gd-birla-group-gandhi-nationalist-freedom-struggle-history/